CONT

Biography of Karl Marx 2

Chapter I: From February to June 1848 4

Chapter II: June 1848 - June 13, 1849 33

Chapter III: June 13, 1849 - March 10, 1850 68

Karl Marx - Class Struggles

Douglas Stones

BIOGRAPHY OF KARL MARX

Karl Marx was born in Trier, Germany, on May 5, 1818. Of Jewish descent, his paternal grandfather, Meier Halevi Marx, was the rabbi of Trier, and his mother, Henrietta Presburg, was also Jewish. However, his father, Heinrich Marx, converted to Christianity, not because he believed in religion, but to continue to practice his profession, since at that time Jews were not free to practice all professions and conduct business transactions.

It is interesting to think that the main author of the working class cause was born into a middle-class Jewish family. The region of Germany where Marx was born and the historical context are fundamental to understand his biography and thought. The fact that his father had to convert to Christianity, the difficulties that Jews experienced just for being Jews, the pre-revolution political context, and the philosophical issues of his time are crucial aspects to understand his work.

In October 1835, Marx entered the University of Bonn to study law at the age of 17. In 1836 Marx's father transferred him to the University of Berlin. That same year Marx and Jenny became engaged to be married. Both Jenny's and Marx's families were not enthusiastic about the couple, which caused the two to take 7 years to finally get married. Their lives were marked by partnership, as Jenny transcribed and translated her husband's works. The two had 7 children, two of whom died of diseases related to the poverty in which they lived.

Karl Marx's major work, entitled "**The Capital**" (*Das Kapital*), took 16 years to complete. During this period he and his family lived through periods of great need and was almost always supported by his main friend and collaborator, Friedrich Engels. His wife, although the daughter of a baron, could not support the large family for long. And despite the recognition the author received after his death, his books did not make much of a stir during publication.

Marx is known as the founder of an area of knowledge within the human sciences. His works deal with history, philosophy, economics, and sociology. Marx's contribution to economics is undeniable, especially regarding the theory of economic value and the development of concepts such as surplus value and the commodity fetish. For history, the materialist conception is considered a watershed. To think a way out of capitalism, seeking new forms of production and economic distribution that would equalize men in their material and social conditions, freeing them from alienation, was one of the greatest efforts of Marx's theory.

Marx's work is almost always analyzed from his intellectual influences, such as Hegel, Fauerbach, Ricardo, and Adam Smith. The scope of his works is immeasurable, but we can cite the Russian Revolution as one of the events related to the impact of his work. His name is invariably associated with theories on communism, socialism, and revolution.

Karl Marx died on March 14, 1883 in London.

CHAPTER I: FROM FEBRUARY TO JUNE 1848

With the exception of a few chapters, every major division of the annals of the revolution from 1848 to 1849 carries the title "Defeat of the revolution!"

In these defeats, it was not the revolution that succumbed. It was the traditional pre-revolutionary appendages, resulting from social relations that had not yet sharpened into violent class contradictions: people, illusions, ideas, projects that the revolutionary party had not developed before the February revolution and which it could not realize with the February victory, but only through a series of defeats.

In a word: it was not by its immediate tragicomic achievements that revolutionary progress opened its way; on the contrary, it was only by bringing about a strong, compact counter-revolution, it was in creating an adversary and fighting it that the party of subversion could finally become a truly revolutionary party.

The purpose of the following pages is to demonstrate how this happened.

The Defeat Of June 1848

After the June revolution, when the liberal banker Laffitte led his compadre, the Duke of Orleans, into the Prefecture in triumph, he let slip these words: "Now is the beginning of the bankers' reign. Laffitte had betrayed the secret of the revolution. The French bourgeoisie did not reign under Louis-Filippe, it was only part of the kingdom: bankers, kings of the stock exchange, kings of the railroads, owners of coal and iron mines, owners of forests, and that part of the landowners connected to them, those who make up the so-called financial aristocracy. It ruled, it dictated the laws to the Chambers, it distributed the public offices, from the ministries to the tobacco shops.

The industrial bourgeoisie proper formed a portion of the official opposition, which is to say that it was a minority in the Chambers. Its opposition became more and more resolute as the development of the hegemony of the financial aristocracy became more evident; after the riots of 1832, 1834 and 1839, which it drowned in blood, it came to believe its hold on the working class assured. Grandin, manufacturer of Rouen, the most fanatical organ of bourgeois reaction, both in the National Constituent and Legislative Assembly, was Guizot's most violent opponent in the Chamber of Deputies. Léon Faucher, known later for his futile efforts to elevate himself to the role of Guizot of the French counter-revolution, in the last days of Louis-Filippe fought at feather strokes on behalf of Industry and against speculation and its government followers. Bastiat, in the name of Bordeaux and all of wine-growing France, was agitating against the dominant system.

The petty bourgeoisie in all its nuances and the peasant class were completely excluded from political power. Finally, there were in the official opposition, or completely outside the legal state, the ideological representatives and spokesmen of the classes we have just mentioned, their scholars, their lawyers, their doctors, etc., those who, after all, were considered to be the "capacities.

From the beginning, financial penury put the July monarchy under the dependence of the upper bourgeoisie. This dependence became the inexhaustible source of increasing financial trouble. It is impossible to subordinate the management of the state to the interest of national production without establishing the balance of the budget, that is, the balance between state expenditures and revenues. And how to establish this equilibrium without reducing the march of the state, that is, without harming interests that were as it were supports of the dominant system, and without reorganizing the tax situation, that is, without throwing a considerable part of the fiscal burden on the shoulders of the big bourgeoisie?

The indebtedness of the state was, quite the contrary, the direct interest of the fraction of the bourgeoisie that governed and legislated with the Chambers. The state deficit was the very object of their speculation and the main source of their enrichment. At the end of each year, a new deficit. After four or five years, a new loan. Now, each new loan provided the aristocracy with a new opportunity to harm the state, which, kept artificially on the verge of bankruptcy, was forced to deal with the bankers under the most unfavorable conditions. Each new loan was a new opportunity to defraud the public, who invested their capital in interest on the State. And this was done with Stock Exchange operations, in whose secrets the Government and the majority of the House were initiated. In general, the instability of public credit and the knowledge of State secrets enabled the bankers, as well as their confreres in the Chambers and on the throne, to bring about extraordinary and sudden fluctuations in the circulation of public securities, the constant result of which could be none other than the ruin of innumerable small capitalists and the fabulously rapid enrichment of the great speculators. If the budget deficit was the direct interest of the fraction of the bourgeoisie in power, it explains why the extraordinary budget, in the last years of Louis-Filipe's government, greatly exceeded the amount reached in Napoleon's time, exceeding four hundred million francs. Moreover, the enormous sums thus passing through the hands of the State gave occasion to fraudulent contracts of consignment, to corruptions, malpractices, and swindles of all kinds. The plundering of the State, on a grand scale, as with loans, was repeated in detail in public works. The relations between the Chamber and the Government were multiplied in the form of relations between certain administrations and certain contractors.

As well as public spending in general and public borrowing, the ruling class also exploited the construction of railroads. The Chambers of Deputies threw the main burdens on the state and assured the speculating financial aristocracy of the golden fruits. We can recall the scandals that broke out in the Chamber of Deputies when it was discovered, by chance, that all the members of the majority, including some of the ministers, were shareholders in the same railroad companies to which they then entrusted, as legislators, the construction of railroads on behalf of the state.

On the other hand, even the smallest financial reform ran into opposition from the bankers. This was the case, for example, with postal reform. Rothschild protested, Did the state have the right to diminish the sources of income that served to cancel the interest on its ever-increasing debt?

The July monarchy was nothing more than a joint stock company founded to exploit the French national wealth, whose dividends were shared among the ministers, the Chambers, two hundred and forty thousand voters and their clientele. Louis-Philippe was the director of this society with Robert Macaire on the throne. Trade, industry, agriculture, navigation, the interests of the industrial bourgeoisie were ceaselessly threatened and harmed by this system. That is why this same industrial bourgeoisie had written on its banner during the July days: Government at a low price.

While the financial aristocracy dictated the laws, directed

the management of the State, held all the constituted public powers, dominated public opinion by force of facts and by the press, in all spheres, from the court to the most notorious taverns, the same prostitution was reproduced, the same shameless cheating, the same thirst for enrichment, not by defending but by concealing the already existing wealth of others: it was above all at the summit of bourgeois society that the indulging of the most unhealthy and the most unregulated ambitions was unleashed and came at every instant into conflict with bourgeois laws themselves; for it is there, where enjoyment becomes infamous, where gold, mud and blood are mingled, that the wealth from gambling inevitably seeks to be realized. The financial aristocracy, both in its economic form and in its enjoyment, is but the resurrection of the proletarian in tatters at the summits of bourgeois society.

As for the parts of the French bourgeoisie that were not in power, it railed against corruption.

The people shouted, "Down with the great thieves! Down with the murderers!" when, in 1847, in the most illustrious theaters of bourgeois society, those scenes were publicly played out that usually accompanied the proletariat in rags in brothels, hospitals and madhouses, before judges, prisons and the scaffold.

The industrial bourgeoisie saw its interests threatened, the petty bourgeoisie was morally indignant, the popular imagination revolted. Paris was flooded with pamphlets: "The Rothschild dynasty", "The Jews, kings of the time", etc., in which the domination of the financial aristocracy was denounced, offended, with more or less spirit.

Nothing for glory! Peace in every corner and forever! War imposes the cost of three and four percent. This is what the France of the Jews of the Stock Exchange had written on its flag. Its foreign policy was also sinking in a series of humiliations of French national feeling, which reacted more vividly than when the annexation of Cracow by Austria had consummated the plunder of Poland, than when Guizot, in the war of the Swiss Sonderbund, had actively sided with the Holy Alliance. The victory of the Swiss liberals in this imitation of war restored confidence to the bourgeois opposition in France, the bloody rebellion of the people at Palermo acted like an electric discharge on the paralyzed mass of the people and aroused their great memories and their revolutionary passions.

Finally, two world economic events precipitated the explosion of the general malaise and matured the discontent to the point of revolt.

Potato disease and the poor harvests of 1845 and 1846 heightened the general effervescence among the people. The rising cost of living in 1847 provoked bloody conflicts in France, as elsewhere on the continent. Faced with the scandalous orgies of the financial aristocracy, it was the people's struggle for the most elementary means of existence! In Buzançais, hunger rioters were executed; in Paris, satiated scoundrels escaped the courts thanks to the royal family!

The second major economic event that hastened the explosion of the revolution was a general crisis of trade and industry in England. Announced already during the autumn of 1845 by the massive defeat of speculators in railway stocks, arrested during 1846 by a series of marginal measures, such as the impending suppression of duane duties on wheat, this defeat was finally triggered in the autumn of 1847 by the bankruptcy of large colonial commissaries in London, which was closely followed by the breakdown of provincial banks and the closing of factories in English industrial districts. The repercussions of the crisis had not yet been exhausted on the continent when the February revolution broke out.

The damage to trade and industry caused by the economic crisis made the omnipotence of the financial aristocracy more unbearable. The bourgeois opposition provoked a campaign of banquets throughout France in favor of a fiscal reform that was to win for itself a majority in the Chambers and overthrow the Ministry of the Stock Exchange. In Paris, the industrial crisis also had the particular consequence of throwing onto the interior commerce a mass of manufacturers and large merchants who, under the conditions of the moment, could no longer do business on the exterior market. They set up large establishments whose competition caused the ruin of countless grocers and shopkeepers. Hence an enormous amount of bankruptcies in this fraction of the Parisian bourgeoisie; hence their revolutionary action in February. It is known how Guizot and the Chambers countered these proposals for reform with ambiguous provocation; that Louis-Filipe decided too late to form a Barrot ministry; that the people and the army came to the fight; that the army was disarmed as a result of the passive attitude of the national guard, and that the July monarchy had to give way.

The provisional government born from the February barricades necessarily reflected in its composition the various parties that divided among themselves the victory. It could only be a compromise between the different classes that had overthrown the July throne together, but whose interests were opposed. It was composed mostly of representatives of the bourgeoisie. The republican petty bourgeoisie was represented by Ledru-Rollin and Flocon; the republican bourgeoisie by people from the National, the dynastic opposition by Crémieux, Dupont de lEure, etc. The working class had only two representatives, Louis Blanc and Albert. Lamartine, finally, in the provisional government, did not represent any real interest, any determined class; he was the February revolution itself, the common uprising with its illusions, its poetry, its imaginary content, and its courses. But at bottom, the spokesman of the February revolution, both by his position and by his opinions, belonged to the bourgeoisie.

If Paris, as a result of political centralization, dominates France, the workers dominate Paris in moments of revolutionary upheavals. The first manifestation of the existence of the Provisional Government was the attempt to evade this predominant influence by launching from an excited Paris an appeal to the cold-bloodedness of France. Lamartine contested the right of the combatants on the barricades to proclaim the Republic, asserting that only the majority of the French had the power to do so: that it was necessary to wait for their vote, that the Parisian proletariat should not stain its victory with a usurpation. The bourgeoisie allows the proletariat nothing but a usurpation: that of the struggle.

On February 25, around noon, the Republic had not yet been proclaimed, yet all the ministries were already divided among the bourgeois elements of the provisional government and among the generals, bankers and lawyers of the National. But this time, the workers were resolved that they would no longer tolerate a flouting similar to that of July 1830. They were ready to start a new fight and impose the Republic by force of arms. It was with this mission that Raspail addressed the Prefecture. In the name of the Parisian proletariat, he ordered the Provisional Government to proclaim the Republic, declaring that if this order of the people was not executed within two hours he would return at the head of two hundred thousand men. The corpses of the combatants had barely cooled, the barricades had not been removed, the workers were still armed, and the only force that could oppose them was the national guard. Under such circumstances, the political considerations and legal scruples of the provisional government suddenly disappeared. The two-hour deadline had not yet run out when all the walls of Paris displayed in giant characters:

"French Republic! Liberty, Equality, Fraternity!"

With the proclamation of the Republic on the basis of universal suffrage, the goals and the strict motives that had launched the bourgeoisie into the February revolution were fading to mere memories. Instead of just a few fractions of the bourgeoisie, it was all the classes of French society that suddenly found themselves projected into the orbit of political power, forced to leave the boxes, the audience, and the gallery to represent themselves on the revolutionary stage! With constitutional kingship, a semblance of public power that arbitrarily opposed bourgeois society, and a whole series of subordinate struggles that this kind of power requires, also disappeared!

By imposing the Republic on the Provisional Government and, through it, on the whole of France, the proletariat immediately put itself in the foreground as an independent party; but in the same move it threw down a challenge to bourgeois France. What it had conquered was the ground for the struggle for its revolutionary emancipation, but not emancipation itself.

It was necessary, on the contrary, that the February Republic should be able to perfect first of all the domination of the bourgeoisie, by bringing, alongside the financial aristocracy, all the capitalist classes into the sphere of political power. Most of the large landowners, the legitimists, were lifted out of the political nullity to which the July monarchy had condemned them. It was not without reason that the Gazette de France had conducted the agitation in agreement with the opposition newspapers; it was not without reason that La Rochejaquelein, in the Chamber, at the session of February 24, had adopted the party of the revolution. By universal suffrage, the nominal proprietors who form the vast majority of the French people, the peasants, were instituted as the arbiters of France's destiny. Finally, the February Republic made bourgeois domination emerge in all its evidence, overthrowing the crown behind which capital was concealed.

In the same way that in the July days the workers had deposed by struggle the bourgeois monarchy, in the February days it was the bourgeois Republic. Just as the July monarchy had to present itself as a monarchy surrounded by republican institutions, the February Republic had to declare itself a republic surrounded by social institutions. The Parisian proletarian imposed this compromise as well.

It was a worker, Marche, who dictated the decree in which

the newly formed Provisional Government pledged to ensure the existence of workers for work, to provide work for all citizens, etc. And as a few days later he forgot these promises and seemed to have lost sight of the proletariat, twenty thousand workers marched on the Prefecture, shouting, "Organization of labor! Constitution of a special ministry of labor!". Against their will, and after long debates, the provisional government appointed a special permanent commission charged with seeking the means of improving the living conditions of the working classes! This commission was made up of delegates from the professional guilds of Paris and chaired by Louís Blanc and Albert. It was assigned the Luxembourg as a session room. In this way, the representatives of the working class found themselves banished from the seat of the provisional government, of which the bourgeois faction retained in its hands the power of the real state and the reins of administration; and next to the ministries of Finance, Commerce, Public Services, next to the Bank and the Stock Exchange, rose a Socialist synagogue whose great priests, Louis Blanc and Albert, had for a mission to discover the promised land, to proclaim the new gospel and to give work to the Parisian proletariat. Unlike any ordinary state power, they had no budget, no executive power. It was with their heads that they were to tear down the pillars of bourgeois society. While Luxemburg was searching for the philosopher's stone, the legal tender was being minted at the Prefecture.

And yet the demands of the Parisian proletariat, insofar as they went beyond the limits of the bourgeois republic, could acquire no other existence than that, nebulous, of Luxembourg.

It was with the bourgeoisie that the workers had made the February Revolution; it was on the side of the bourgeoisie that they had sought to make their interests prevail; just as it had been with the bourgeois majority that they had installed a worker in the provisional government itself. Organization of labor! But it is the wage earner who is the actual existing bourgeois organization of labor. Without him, no capital, no bourgeoisie, no bourgeois society. A special ministry of labor! But aren't the ministries of Finance, Commerce and Public Services the ministries of bourgeois Labor? By their side, a proletarian Labor ministry could only be a ministry of Impotence, a ministry of Pious Promises, a Luxembourg commission. Just as the workers believed to emancipate themselves alongside the bourgeoisie, so they thought to carry out a proletarian revolution alongside other bourgeois nations and within the national borders of France. But France's conditions of production are determined by her foreign trade, her position in the world market, and the laws of the latter. How would France break them without a European revolutionary war awaited, as compensation, by England, the despot of the world market?

A class which concentrates in itself the revolutionary interests of society, from the instant it revolts finds immediately in its own situation the content and matter of its revolutionary activity: crushing its enemies, taking the measures imposed by the needs of the struggle; and it is the consequences of its own acts that propel it forward. It does not indulge in any theoretical research into its own mission. The French working class had not yet reached that point; it was unable yet to consummate its own revolution.

The development of the industrial proletariat has for general condition the development of the industrial bourgeoisie. It is only under the domination of the latter that its existence takes on a national amplitude enabling it to raise its revolution to the level of a national revolution; it is only then that it, the industrial proletariat, creates itself the modern means of production which become also the means of its revolutionary liberation. Only the domination of the industrial bourgeoisie extirpates the material roots of feudal society and prepares the ground on which a proletarian revolution is possible. French industry is more evolved and the French bourgeoisie more developed from the revolutionary point of view than that of the rest of the continent. But wasn't the February revolution directly directed against the financial aristocracy? This fact proved that the industrial bourgeoisie of France did not reign. The industrial bourgeoisie can only reign where modern industry has shaped all property relations in its own way; and industry can only acquire this power where it has conquered the world market, because national borders are not sufficient for its development. Now, French industry remains largely owner of the world market only thanks to a prohibitive system subject to more or less important modifications. If, consequently, the French proletariat possesses, at the time of a revolution in Paris, a real power and influence which incite it to fight beyond its strength, in the rest of France it is concentrated in a few scattered points where industry is centralized, and disappears almost completely under the superior number of peasants and petty bourgeois. The struggle against capital, developed under the modern form, in its fullness which is the struggle of the industrial wage-earner against the industrial bourgeoisie, was in France a partial fact which, after the February days, could nourish the national content of the revolution even less, since the struggle against the lower forms of exploitation of capital, the struggle of the peasants against the usury of the mortgage, of the petty bourgeois against the big merchant, the banker and the manufacturer - in short, against bankruptcy -, was still sunk in the general revolt against the financial aristocracy in general. It is also easily explained that the Paris proletariat sought to make its interests triumph over the interests of the bourgeoisie instead of claiming them as the revolutionary interests of society itself, and that it brought down the red flag before the tricolour flag The French workers could not take a single step forward, nor touch a single hair of the bourgeois regime, before the other classes placed between the proletariat and the bourgeoisie - peasants and petty bourgeois revolted against that regime, against the domination of capital - had been forced by the march of the revolution to ally themselves with the proletarians, its vanguard. It was only by the stunning defeat of June that the workers were able to win this victory.

The Luxembourg commission, this creation of the Paris workers, has the merit of having revealed, from the top of a European tribune, the secret of the 19th century revolution: the emancipation of the proletariat. The Moniteur exploded when it had to officially disseminate the "disordered exaltations" which, until then, had been buried in the apocryphal works of the socialists and which, like the distant legends half terrifying, half ridiculous, only came from time to time to ring in the ears of the bourgeoisie. Europe awoke startled, in the surprise of its bourgeois numbness. Thus, in the spirit of the proletarians who had always confused the financial aristocracy with the bourgeoisie, in the imagination of brave republicans who had even denied the existence of classes or admitted it at most as a consequence of constitutional monarchy, in the hypocritical words of bourgeois fractions that had been excluded from power until then, the domination of the bourgeoisie had been abolished with the establishment of the Republic. All the monarchists then became republicans and all the millionaires of Paris became workers. The word that corresponded to this imaginary elimination of class relations was fraternity; universal fraternity and brotherhood. Harmless denial of class antagonists, sentimental balance between contradictory class interests, enthusiastic exaltation above class struggle, fraternity was really the motto of the February revolution. It was a simple misunderstanding that separated the classes, and on February 24, Lamartine christened the provisional government, "A government that ends this terrible misunderstanding that exists between the different classes." The proletariat of Paris was carried away into this generous intoxication of fraternity.

For its part, the provisional government, once forced to proclaim the Republic, did everything to make it acceptable to the bourgeoisie and the provinces. The bloody horrors of the first French Republic were condemned with the abolition of the death penalty for political crime; the press was liberated for any kind of opinion; the army, the courts and the administration remained, with a few exceptions, in the hands of their former dignitaries; no explanations were demanded from any of the great culprits of the July monarchy. The bourgeois Republicans of the National were amusing themselves by exchanging the names and clothes of the monarchy for those of the old Republic. In their eyes, the Republic was nothing but a new ball gown for old bourgeois society. The main merit of the young Republic was that it frightened no one, but rather continually frightened itself, and by its meekness, its passive life, it won the right to life and the disarmament of resistance. To the privileged classes in the interior, to the despotic powers abroad, it was loudly proclaimed that the Republic was of a peaceful nature: live and let live was its motto. Moreover, shortly after the February revolution, the Germans, the Poles, the Austrians, the Dutch, the Italians revolted, each people according to its own situation. Russia and England had not yet come so far; the former was contained by terror, while the latter was in a state of boiling. The Republic, then, did not see a single enemy nation before it. Thus, no great external complications that could rekindle the flames, precipitate the revolutionary process, push the provisional government forward or, if need be, throw it overboard. The Parisian proletariat, which saw in the Republic its own creation, naturally acclaimed every act of the Provisional Government that allowed it to take its place more easily in bourgeois society. It meekly allowed itself to be employed by Caussidière as a policeman to protect property in Paris, just as it allowed the wage disputes between workers and employers to be settled amicably by Louis Blanc. He considered it essential to keep the bourgeois honor of the Republic immaculate in the eyes of Europe.

The Republic met no resistance inside or outside. That is what disarmed it. Its mission was not to revolutionarily transform the world; it consisted only in adapting itself to the conditions of bourgeois society. Nothing testifies more eloquently to the fanaticism with which the Provisional Government indulged in such a mission than the financial measures it took.

Public credit and private credit were naturally shaken. Public credit is based on the belief that the state lets itself be exploited by the Jews of Finance. But the old state had disappeared and the revolution was directed first and foremost against the financial aristocracy. The swings of the last commercial crisis in Europe were not yet over. Bankruptcies still followed one another.

Private credit was then paralyzed, circulation slack, production stagnant, before the February revolution exploded. The revolutionary crisis intensified the commercial crisis. Now, private credit is based on the belief that bourgeois production in the whole range of its relations, the bourgeois order, is inviolate and inviolable. What should not be the effect of a revolution that called into question the foundation of bourgeois production, the economic slavery of the proletariat, and deciphered the sphinx of Luxembourg face to face? The revolt of the proletariat is the suppression of bourgeois credit, because it is the suppression of bourgeois production and its regime. Public credit and private credit are the economic thermometer to measure the intensity of a revolution. As they, the credits, fall, the feverish ardor and the creative force of the revolution rise.

The Provisional Government wanted to strip the Republic of its anti-bourgeois appearance. It needed first of all to secure the exchange value of this new form of State, its price on the stock exchange. With the current price of the Republic on the stock exchange, private credit necessarily rose again.

To dispel even the suspicion that it was unwilling or unable to meet the obligations bequeathed by the monarchy, to restore confidence in bourgeois morality, in the solvency of the Republic, the Provisional Government resorted to a braggadocio as puerile as it was undignified. Before the legal due date, it paid the state's creditors the interest of five, four and a half and four percent. The bourgeois arrogance, the security of the capitalists were awakened abruptly when they saw the eager haste with which it sought to buy their confidence.

The financial embarrassment of the Provisional Government was not eased by this coup de théâtre that deprived it of the few resources available. Financial penury could no longer be concealed, and it was up to the petty bourgeoisie, employees and workers to pay for the pleasant surprise made to the state's creditors.

Savings accounts in excess of one hundred francs were declared to be non-reimbursable in cash. The amounts deposited in savings accounts were confiscated and converted, by decree, into a non-repayable state debt. The petty bourgeois, already badly treated, became irritated with the Republic. Receiving Treasury bonds instead of his savings account, he was forced to go and sell them on the Stock Exchange and deliver himself into the hands of the Jews of the Stock Exchange, the same ones against whom he had made the February revolution.

The financial aristocracy, which reigned in the July monarchy, had its cathedral in the Bank. Just as the Stock Exchange manages public credit, the Bank governs commercial credit.

Directly threatened by the February revolution, not only in its domination, but in its entire existence, the Bank applied itself, from the beginning, to discredit the Republic by generalizing the suspension of credit. It abruptly suspended all credit to bankers and merchants. Since this maneuver did not provoke an immediate counter-revolution, the Bank directed its counter-strike against itself. The capitalists withdrew the money they had deposited in their cellars. The holders of bank notes rushed to their boxes to exchange them for gold and cash.

The Provisional Government could, without resorting to violence, legally bankrupt the Bank; it was enough for it to maintain a passive attitude and abandon the Bank to its own fate. The bankruptcy of the Bank was the deluge sweeping in a flash from French soil the financial aristocracy, the strongest and most dangerous enemy of the Republic, the golden pedestal of the July monarchy. Once the Bank was bankrupt, the bourgeoisie would be forced to consider as a last desperate attempt at salvation the creation by the government of a national bank and the subordination of national credit to the control of the nation.

The Provisional Government, on the contrary; gave forced course to the bank notes. It did even better. It turned all the provincial banks into branches of the Bank of France, allowing it to cast its net over the entire country. Later, he pledged the patrimonial forests as collateral for the loan made with the Bank. This is how the February revolution directly consolidated and expanded the "bancocracy" it was supposed to destroy.

In the meantime, the Provisional Government was dragging itself through the nightmare of a growing deficit. It begged in vain for patriotic sacrifices. Only the workers were giving it their alms. It was necessary to resort to a heroic measure, the enactment of a new tax. But on whom? The wolves of the Stock Exchange, the kings of the Bank, the creditors of the State, the capitalists, the industrialists? It was not a way to make the bourgeoisie quietly accept the Republic. It was, on the one hand, to jeopardize the credit of the State and the credit of commerce, which one was trying to buy at the price of such great sacrifices, such great humiliations. But someone had to pay. And who was the one sacrificed to bourgeois credit? Jacques Bonhomme, the peasant.

The Provisional Government established an additional tax of forty-five cents per franc on the four direct taxes. The government press tried to make the proletariat of Paris believe that this tax would preferably affect the large landed property, the owners of the billion granted by the Restoration. But in reality, the tax affected first and foremost the peasant class, which is the vast majority of the French people. It was they who had to pay the expenses of the February revolution, it was they who were the main support of the counter-revolution. The forty-five cent tax was a matter of life and death for the French peasant; it made it a matter of life and death for the Republic. The Republic for the peasant of France was henceforth the forty-five cent tax; and in the proletariat of Paris he saw the squanderer who amused himself at his expense.

While the revolution of 1789 had started by freeing the peasants from feudal burdens, the revolution of 1848 heralded a new tax on the rural population in order not to endanger capital and to ensure the functioning of the state mechanism.

The only means by which the Provisional Government could dispose of all these inconveniences and get the State out of its old ways was by declaring the State bankrupt. It is remembered how in the National Assembly Ledru-Rollin was seized, too late, of a virtuous indignation, declaring that he refused this suggestion of the Scholar Jew Fould, made Minister of Finance. Fould had extended to him the fruit of the tree of wisdom.

Recognizing the debts that the old bourgeois society had thrown at the state, the Provisional Government retreated to its discretion. It had become the embarrassed debtor of bourgeois society, instead of standing up as the threatening creditor who had to recover revolutionary debts going back many years. It was necessary for him to consolidate the faltering bourgeois relations in order to free himself from obligations that could only be fulfilled within the framework of these relations. Credit became a condition of his existence, and the concessions, the promises made to the proletariat, chains he needed to break. Even the simple expression "emancipation of the workers" represented an intolerable danger for the new Republic, because it was a permanent protest against the re-establishment of the confidence that rests on the uninterrupted and unalterable recognition of the existing economic class relations. It was necessary then to break with the workers.

The February revolution had thrown the army out of Paris. The National Guard, that is, the bourgeoisie in its various guises, constituted the only force. Nevertheless, it felt itself to be intimately inferior to the proletariat. Moreover, it was forced, not without opposing the most tenacious resistance, not without creating hundreds of obstacles, to gradually open its ranks to allow the armed proletarians to enter. There was then only one way out: to play one part of the proletariat off against the other.

To this end, the Provisional Government formed twenty-four battalions for the protection of the territory, each with a thousand men, composed of young men between fifteen and twenty years of age. They belonged for the most part to the ragged proletariat, which in all the large cities constitutes a crowd distinctly different from the industrial proletariat: barns of thieves and criminals, of all kinds, living refuse of society, individuals without legal professions, vagrants, without dignity and without a roof, different according to the degree of culture of the region to which they belonged, but always presenting the character of lazzaroni. As it turned out that the Provisional Government recruited them very young, they were absolutely influential and capable of the greatest acts of heroism and the most exalted self-sacrifice, but also of the most sordid banditry and the most disgraceful venality. The Provisional Government paid them at a rate of one franc fifty a day, or rather, bought them. It gave them a special uniform, that is, it differentiated them outwardly from the workers in overalls. As chiefs, they were given officers from the standing army, or else chiefs elected by themselves, young sons of the bourgeoisie whose braggadocio about death for the fatherland and devotion to the Republic seduced them.

It was thus that he had, in the face of the Paris proletariat, an army drawn from its own midst, strong, of twenty-four thousand young, robust men, of a mad temerity. The proletariat acclaimed the garde mobile during its marches through Paris. They recognized in it their vanguard fighters on the barricades. It considered it the proletarian guard, in opposition to the bourgeois national guard. His mistake was forgivable.

In addition to the garde mobile, the government also decided to gather around itself an army of industrial workers. Hundreds of thousands of workers, thrown out into the streets by the crisis and the revolution, were recruited by Minister Maríe for the so-called national workshops. Under this pompous name was concealed only the occupation of laborers in tedious, monotonous and unproductive backfill work in exchange for a salary of twenty-three sous. English open-air workhouses, that's what these national workshops were. And nothing more. The Provisional Government believed that with these workshops it had formed a second proletarian army against the workers themselves. But this time the bourgeoisie was wrong about these national workshops, just as the workers had been wrong about the garde mobile. The bourgeoisie had created an army for rebellion.

However, one goal was being achieved.

National workshops, that is what the popular workshops advocated by Louis Blanc in Luxembourg were called. Marie's workshops, conceived in direct opposition to Luxembourg, by their common insignia gave rise to plots whose equivocations were worthy of the jacks of Spanish comedy. The Provisional Government, itself, secretly spread the rumor that these national workshops were an invention of Louis Blanc, which seemed all the more credible since Louis Blanc, the prophet of the national workshops, was a member of the Provisional Government. And in the confusion armed, half naively, half intentionally, by the Parisian bourgeoisie, in the opinion in which France and Europe were artificially kept, these work-houses were the first realization of socialism, which with them was tied to the pillory.

It was not by their content, but by their title, that the national workshops gave consistency to the protest of the proletariat against bourgeois industry, against bourgeois credit and against the bourgeois Republic. It was then that all the hatred of the bourgeoisie fell upon the national workshops. It had found at the same time the point on which to direct its attack, once it was sufficiently strengthened to break openly with the illusions of February. All the uneasiness and all the bitterness of the petty bourgeois turned at the same moment against the national workshops, this common target. It was with real fury that they calculated the sums absorbed by those lazy proletarians while their own lot became more intolerable every day. A state allowance for a make-believe job, that's what socialism was, they snarled to themselves. The national workshops, Luxemburg's speeches, workers' parades all over Paris, this is where they were looking for the cause of their misery. And no one was more fanatical against the supposed machinations of the communists than the petty bourgeois, desperately pushed into bankruptcy.

Thus, in the ever closer body to body between the bourgeoisie and the proletariat, the former had in its hands all the advantages, all the decisive posts, all the middle layers of society, at the very moment when the waves of the February revolution were breaking over the entire continent; when every mailbag carried a new revolutionary pamphlet, whether from Italy, Germany, or the far reaches of southeastern Europe, and fed the general intoxication of the people by giving them continuous testimonies of a victory that they had already consummated.

On March 17 and April 16 the first battles of the outposts of the great class struggle hidden under the wings of the bourgeois Republic took place.

March 17 revealed the equivocal situation of the proletariat which did not permit any decisive act. Its demonstration, at its origins, was intended to lead the Provisional Government back to the path of revolution, to achieve, according to circumstances, the exclusion of its bourgeois members, and to demand the postponement of the date of the elections to the National Assembly and the national guard. But on March 16 the bourgeoisie, represented by the national guard, made a hostile demonstration to the Provisional Government. To cries of "Down with Ledru-Rollín!" it marched on City Hall. And on March 17 the people were forced to shout "Vila LedruRollin!", "Long live the Provisional Government!" It was forced to take, against the bourgeoisie, the side of the bourgeois Republic whose existence seemed to it to be in question. The people consolidated the government rather than defeating it. March 17 led to melodrama, and when the proletariat of Paris displayed its gigantic body once more on that day, the bourgeoisie, that which was part of and that which was not part of the Provisional Government, was more than resolved to crush it.

On April 16 the Provisional Government, in connivance with the bourgeoisie, set up a mess. The workers had gathered in large numbers on the Champ-de-Mars and at the hippodrome to prepare for the elections of the general staff of the National Guard. Suddenly, from one end of Paris to the other, with the speed of lightning, the rumor spread that the workers were gathered with guns on the Champ-de-Mars, under the command of Louis Blanc, Blanqui, Cabet, and Raspail, to go to the Prefecture, overthrow the provisional government, and proclaim a communist government. The general alert sounded. Ledru-Rollin, Marrast, Lamartine later disputed the honor of this initiative: within an hour, one hundred thousand men were at arms, the Prefecture was occupied at every point by national guards; all over Paris echoed the cries of "Down with the Communists! Down with Louis Blanc, Blanqui, Raspail, Cabet!". A world of delegations come to bring their solidarity to the Provisional Government, all ready to save the fatherland and society. When the workers finally appear before the City Hall to hand the Provisional Government a patriotic collection made on the Champ-de-Mars, they are astonished to learn that bourgeois Paris, in a simulacrum of combat organized in the utmost seriousness, has warred its own shadow.

The "terrible" attack of April 16 provided the pretext for calling the army back to Paris - the real purpose of the crudely mounted comedy - as well as sparking reactionary Federalist demonstrations in the province.

On May 4, the National Assembly met as the result of general elections with direct universal suffrage. Universal suffrage no longer had the magical virtue that older republicans had attributed to it. Throughout France, or at least in most of France, the French saw the citizens as having the same interests, the same judgment, etc. Such was their cult of the people. But instead of the imaginary people, elections are aimed sharply at the real people, that is, the representatives of the different classes into which they are subdivided. We have seen why peasants and petty bourgeois had to vote under the command of the bourgeoisie entirely in the heat of the struggle and of the large landlords impatient for restoration. But if universal suffrage was not the miraculous magic wand by which brave republicans had taken it, it had the infinitely greater merit of unleashing the class struggle, of making the different middle layers of petty-bourgeois society quickly lose their illusions and their disappointments in the face of the trials of life, to raise all the factions of the class of the exploiters to the summit of power in one fell swoop, and thus tear off their deceptive masks, while the monarchy, with its censorious system, only allowed certain factions of the bourgeoisie to be compromised and kept the others discreetly, in the wings, girding them with the halo of a common opposition.

In the national constituent assembly that met on May 4, the bourgeois republicans, the republicans of the National, commanded. The legitimists and the Orleanists dared not show themselves first except under the mask of bourgeois republicanism. It was only in the name of the Republic that the struggle against the proletariat could be initiated.

It is May 4th, and not February 25th, that dates the Republic, better said, the Republic recognized by the French people, and not the Republic imposed by the Parisian proletariat on the provisional government, not the Republic of social institutions, not the oneiric image that passed before the eyes of the combatants on the barricades. The Republic proclaimed by the National Assembly, the only legitimate one, is the Republic which is not a revolutionary weapon against the bourgeois order, which is above all the political reconstitution, the political consolidation of bourgeois society; in short, the bourgeois Republic. This is what is stated loud and clear on the rostrum of the National Assembly. And the entire bourgeois press, both republican and anti-republican, makes a chorus.

And we saw how the February Republic was in reality, and could not be, anything but a bourgeois Republic; how, on the other hand, the Provisional Government was, by direct pressure from the proletariat, compelled to proclaim it a Republic endowed with social institutions; how the Parisian proletarian was already capable of going beyond the bourgeois Republic in ways other than in idea, in imagination; how, everywhere he actually went into action, it was to render service to it, to the Republic; how the promises that had been made to him became an unbearable danger in the new Republic; and how the whole existence of the Provisional Government was reduced to a continuous struggle against the claims of the proletariat.

In the National Assembly, it was the whole of France that made itself the judge of the Parisian proletariat. She immediately broke with the social illusions of the February revolution, promptly proclaimed the bourgeois republic and only the bourgeois republic. She immediately excluded from the executive committee that appointed the representatives of the proletariat: Louis Blanc and Albert. She rejected the proposal for a special ministry of Labor. She received with a storm of applause the statement of Minister Trelat: "It is not a question of anything else but to return labor to its old conditions."

But all this was not enough. The February Republic had been won by the workers with the passive help of the bourgeoisie. The proletarians rightfully considered themselves the victors of February and had the arrogant pretensions of the victors. It was necessary for them to be defeated in the streets, it was necessary to show them that they would succumb the moment they fought, not with the bourgeoisie, but against it. Just as the February Republic, with its socialist concessions, needed a battle of the proletariat united with the bourgeoisie, against the monarchy, so a second battle was needed to liberate the Republic from its socialist concessions, to highlight the bourgeois Republic, to show it officially holding power. It was with arms in hand that the bourgeoisie was to reject the demands of the proletariat. And the real birthplace of the bourgeois Republic is not the February victory, it is the June defeat.

The proletariat precipitated the decision when, on May 15, it stormed the National Assembly, trying in vain to regain its revolutionary influence, with no other result than that of taking its determined leaders to the jails of the bourgeoisie. "It must be stopped!" With this cry the National Assembly gave free rein to its resolution to force the proletariat into decisive combat. The Executive Committee promulgated a series of provocative decrees, such as the ban on popular demonstrations, etc. From the rostrum of the National Constituent Assembly, the workers were directly provoked, reviled, harassed. But the point of attack, as we have seen, was still the national workshops. It was with them in mind that the Constituent Assembly categorically indicated to the Executive Committee to only wait for the moment to hear its own project transformed into an order of the National Assembly.

The Executive Committee began by making admission to the national workshops more difficult, by changing the daily wage into a production wage, by exiling to Sologne workers who were not born in Paris, under the pretext of having them perform backfill work. These landfill jobs were in reality only a rhetorical formula with which to prepare their exile, as already disillusioned workers taught their comrades. Finally, on June 21, a decree appeared in the Moniteur ordering the brutal dismissal of all single workers from the national workshops or their enlistment in the army.

The workers no longer had a choice: either they starved to

death or they began the struggle. They responded, on June 22, with the formidable insurrection where the first great battle between the two classes that divide modern society took place. It was a struggle for the maintenance or the extermination of the bourgeois order. The veil that hid the Republic was torn.

It is known that the workers, with unparalleled courage and talent, without leaders, without a common plan, without resources, most without weapons, stood up to the army, the garde mobile, the national guard that flocked from the province for five days. It is known that the bourgeoisie took revenge for their mortal anguish with an astonishing brutality and massacred more than three thousand prisoners.

The official representatives of French democracy were so attached to republican ideology that it took them several weeks to begin to suspect what the June fight was all about. They were dumbstruck by the cloud of dust in which their imaginary Republic was disappearing.

As for the direct impression that the new June defeat produced on us, the reader will allow us to describe it in the terms of the Norva Gazeta Renana (Neue Rheinische Zeitung):

"The last official vestige of the February revolution, the Executive Committee, dissipated like a ghost before the gravity of events. The luminous rockets of Lamartine have become the incendiary fires of Cavaignac. The fraternity of antagonistic classes in which one exploits the other, that fraternity proclaimed in February, inscribed in large letters on the foreheads of Paris, in every prison, in every barrack, its true, authentic, prosaic expression, is the civil war, the civil war in its most terrible form, the war between labor and capital. This fraternity shone in all the windows of Paris on the evening of June 25, when bourgeois Paris was glowing, while proletarian Paris was burning, bleeding, agonizing. The fraternity lasted only as long as the interests of the bourgeoisie were brothers to the interests of the proletariat. Pedants of the old revolutionary tradition of 1793, socialist theoreticians, begging for the people from the bourgeoisie, and who were allowed to preach long homilies and commit themselves for as long as necessary to keep the proletarian lion asleep; republicans who claimed all the old bourgeois order but the crowned head; people of the dynastic opposition for whom chance substituted the overthrow of a dynasty for the exchange of a ministry; legitimists who wished not to get rid of their uniforms but to change their cut... These were the allies with whom the people made their February. The February revolution was the beautiful revolution, the revolution of general sympathy, because the antagonisms that flickered then against royalty slept, embryonic, side by side; because the social struggle that made its second plane had only acquired a vaporous existence, the existence of the phrase, of the verb. The June revolution is the odious revolution, the repugnant revolution, because reality has taken the place of discourse, because the Republic has laid bare the head of the monster, knocking down the crown that protected and hid it. Order! This was Guizot's battle cry. Order! cried Sebastiani, this Guizot in a minor way, when Warsaw became Russian. Order! cried Cavaignac, a brutal echo of the French National Assembly and the Republican bourgeoisie. Order! thundered the machine-gun fire, shattering the body of the proletariat. None of the numerous revolutions of the French bourgeoisie after 1789 was an attack on order, because each one of them let class domination subsist, let workers' slavery subsist, let the bourgeois order subsist, every time the political form of that domination and slavery was changed. June came to damage this order. Cursed be June! "(Neue Rheinische Zeitung, June 29, 1848).

Damn June! repeats the echo from France.

It was the bourgeoisie that led the proletariat to the June insurrection. Hence his condemnation. His recognized immediate needs did not impel him to the desire to obtain by violence the downfall of the bourgeoisie, he did not yet possess the capacity for such a task. The Moniteur had to teach him officially that the times were no longer those the Republic thought they were, in order to pay homage to its illusions; only defeat persuaded him of this truth that the slightest improvement in his situation remained a utopia within the bourgeois Republic, a utopia which becomes a crime the moment it wants to become real. His demands, excessive in form, puerile in content - and for this very reason still bourgeois - with which he wanted to wrest permission for the February revolution, were replaced by the audacious slogan of the revolutionary struggle: Overthrow of the bourgeoisie! Dictatorship of the working class!

Making its grave the cradle of the bourgeois republic, the proletariat has forced this same bourgeois republic to appear immediately in its pure form as the state whose avowed aim is to eternalize the denomination of capital, the slavery of labor. The eyes always fixed on the scarred, implacable, invincible enemy - because its existence, for him, is the condition of his own life, for her - bourgeois domination, freed from any hindrance, was to be immediately transformed into bourgeois terrorism. Once the proletariat was removed from the scene, and the dictatorship of the bourgeoisie officially recognized, the middle layers of bourgeois society, the petty bourgeoisie and the peasant class, as their situation became more unbearable and their opposition to the bourgeoisie rougher, would ally themselves more and more with the proletariat. The cause of their misery they had found in its progress; they were now to find it in its downfall.

When the June insurrection strengthened, throughout the continent, the security of the bourgeoisie and led it to openly ally with the feudal royalty against the people, who was the first victim of this union? The continental bourgeoisie itself. The defeat of June prevented it from securing its domination and from making the people stop, half satisfied, half discontented, at the lowest level of the bourgeois revolution.

Finally, the defeat of June revealed to the despotic powers of Europe a secret: France had, whatever the cost, to maintain peace abroad in order to be able to bring civil war to the interior.

Thus the peoples who had begun the struggle for their national independence were handed over to the supremacy of Russia, Austria and Prussia, but at the same time these national revolutions whose fate was subordinated to that of the proletarian revolution were deprived of their apparent autonomy, of their independence in the face of the great social subversion. The Hungarian must not be free, nor the Polish, nor the Italian, as long as the worker remains a slave!

Finally, the victories of the Holy Alliance have given Europe such a shape that any new proletarian uprising in France will immediately be the sign of a world war. The new French revolution will soon be obliged to abandon the national terrain and conquer the European terrain, the only one where the social revolution of the 19th century could take it. So it was only by the defeat of June that the conditions were created which enabled France to take the initiative in the European revolution. It was only bathed in the blood of the June insurrectionists that the tricolor flag became the flag of the European revolution, the red flag.

And we shouted: The revolution is dead! Long live the revolution!

CHAPTER II: JUNE 1848 - JUNE 13, 1849

The 25th of February 1848 gave France the Republic, the 25th of June imposed the revolution. After June, revolution meant: overthrow of bourgeois society, when, before February, the word meant: overthrow of the State form.

The June fight had been directed by the republican fraction of the bourgeoisie; with the victory, the power of the State was necessarily returned to them. The state of siege placed Paris at its feet, without resistance, and in the provinces a moral state of siege reigned, the arrogance of victory filled with menacing brutality and the fanatical love of property unleashed among the peasants. Danger in sight!

As well as the revolutionary power of the workers, the political influence of the Democratic Republicans crumbled, or rather, the Republicans in the petty-bourgeois sense, represented in the Executive Committee by Ledru-Rollin, in the National Constituent Assembly by the party of La Mantagne, in the press by La Réjorme. In agreement with the bourgeois republicans, on April 16 they had conspired against the proletariat; during the June days they had fought together. Thus they themselves were destroying the background on which their party was outlining itself as a force, because the petty bourgeoisie can only maintain a revolutionary position vis-à-vis the bourgeoisie when it has the proletariat behind it. They were dismissed. The simulacrum of alliance, made with them begrudgingly, covertly, at the time of the Provisional Government and the Executive Committee, was broken publicly by the bourgeois republicans.

Scorned and repulsed as allies, they were reduced to the lower level of mere satellites of the tricolor republicans from whom they could extract no concessions, but whose domination they were encouraged to support whenever this domination, and with it the Republic itself, seemed called into question by the anti-republican factions of the bourgeoisie. These factions, finally, the Orleanists and the legitimists, were from the beginning in the minority in the National Constituent Assembly. Before the June days, they did not dare to react on their own except under the mask of bourgeois republicanism. The June victory led to Cavaignac being hailed for a moment as the savior of all bourgeois France, and when, immediately after the June days, the anti-republican party recovered its independence, the military dictatorship and the state of siege in Paris did not allow it to put out its antennae except very timidly and cautiously.

Since 1830, the republican fraction of the bourgeoisie, its - writers, its spokesmen, its "capacities," its deputies, generals, bankers and lawyers, had united around a Parisian newspaper, the National, which had secondary editions in the province. The National group was the dynasty of the tricolor republic. It immediately seized all the public functions, the ministries, the General Police Board, the mayor's offices, the highest posts made vacant in the army. At the head of the executive power was his general, Cavaignac. Its editor-in-chief, Marrast, became the permanent president of the national constituent assembly. At the same time, in its halls, master of ceremonies, he did the honors of the legal Republic.

Even the French revolutionary writers, out of a sort of coyness in the face of republican tradition, gave credence to the error that the monarchists had predominated in the National Constituent Assembly. After the June days, on the contrary, the Constituent Assembly became the exclusive representation of bourgeois republicanism, and this aspect became more and more firmly established as the influence of the tricolor republicans outside the Assembly crumbled. It was a matter of defending the form of the bourgeois republic, they had the votes of the democratic republicans; it was a matter of its content, their very way of speaking no longer distinguished them from the bourgeois monarchist fractions, because it is precisely the interests of the bourgeoisie, the material conditions of its domination and its class exploitation that form the content of the bourgeois republic.

So it was not monarchy, but republicanism that was being realized in the life and acts of this Constituent Assembly that ended, not by dying or being killed, but by beginning to rot.

During the entire period of her domination, while she represented on the stage the morceau de bravoure of the gallant, an uninterrupted holocaust was taking place in the background: serial convictions, under martial law, of the June insurgents taken prisoner or their deportation without trial. The Constituent Assembly had the tact to recognize that in the June insurgents it was not the criminals it was judging, but the enemies it was crushing.

The first act of the national constituent assembly was to set up a commission of inquiry into the events of June and May 15 and into the participation of the leaders of the Socialist and Democratic parties on those days. The inquiry was directed, directly, against Louis Blanc, Ledru-Rollin and Caussidiére. The bourgeois Republicans were burning with impatience to get rid of these rivals. They could not entrust the execution of their revenge to anyone more qualified than Monsieur Odilon Barrot, the former leader of the dynastic opposition, liberalism in the form of a man, the "grave nullity," innate mediocrity; he had not only a dynasty to avenge, but bills to demand from the revolutionaries for a lost ministry presidency, a sure guarantee of his inflexibility. It was then this Barrot who was appointed president of the commission of inquiry, and he formed piece by piece, against the February revolution, a complete process which can be summarized thus: March 17, demonstration; April 16, plot; May 15, attack; June 23, civil war! Why didn't he extend his wise research to February 24? The Journal de débats gave the answer: February 24 is the "foundation of Rome"! The origin of the states is lost in a myth that is to be believed without discussion. Louis Blanc and Caussidière were handed over to the courts. The National Assembly was consummating its own purification, which it had begun on May 15.

The capital tax project, conceived by the Provisional Government and taken up by Goudchaux - in the form of a mortgage tax - was rejected by the Constituent Assembly; the law limiting working time to ten hours was repealed, imprisonment for debt was reinstated. The majority of the French population, those who could neither read nor write, were barred from the jury. Why not also the right to vote? The bond for newspapers was reinstated, the right of association restricted.

But in their haste to restore to the old bourgeois relations the old guarantees, and to make all traces left by the revolutionary waves disappear, the bourgeois republicans ran into a resistance whose threat constituted an unexpected danger.

No one, in the June days, had fought more fanatically for the safeguarding of property and the re-establishment of credit than the Parisian petty bourgeois, café owners, restaurant owners, wine merchants, small shopkeepers, artisans, etc. Gathering all their forces, the store had marched against the barricade to re-establish the circulation leading from the street to the store. But behind the barricade were the customers and the debtors; before it, the store's creditors. And when the barricades were torn down and the workers crushed, when the guardians of the department stores, in the drunkenness of victory, rushed back to their stores, they found their entrances blocked by a savior of property, an official credit agent who presented them with his comminatory bonds: overdue bill, overdue term, overdue promissory note, store down, shopkeeper down.

Safeguarding property! But the house they lived in was not their property, the store they kept was not their property, the goods they sold were not their property. Neither their trade, nor the plate they ate on, nor the bed they slept in belonged to them. It was precisely in their face that this property was to be saved, for the benefit of the landlord who had rented the house, the banker who had discounted the bills, the capitalist who had made the cash advances, the manufacturer who had entrusted these shopkeepers with the goods to be sold, the big merchant who had given these craftsmen the credit for the raw materials. Re-establishment of credit! But once consolidated, credit showed itself to be an active and zealous god, precisely by throwing out of its four walls the insolvent debtor with his wife and children, by handing over his supposed fortune to capital, and by taking to prison for debts the one who had risen again, menacingly, over the corpses of the June insurrectionists.

The petty bourgeois realized, terrified, that they had given themselves up without resistance into the hands of their creditors by crushing the workers. Their bankruptcy, chronic since February and apparently ignored, was declared public after June.

They had left them their nominal property only time to be thrown on the battlefield in the name of ownership. Now that the great matter of the proletariat had been settled, one could equally settle, in turn, the small account of the grocer. In Paris, the total of overdue securities amounted to more than twenty-one million francs; in the provinces, more than eleven million. The holders of commercial leases on more than seven thousand Parisian houses had not paid their rent after February.

If the National Assembly had made an inquiry into the political debt going back to February, the petty bourgeois were now asking, for their part, for an inquiry into the civil debts up to February 24. They gathered en masse in the hall of the Stock Exchange, and for every merchant who was able to prove that he had not gone bankrupt for any reason other than as a result of the interruption of business caused by the February revolution, and that his business was going well on February 24, they demanded with threats an extension of his due dates by a judgment of the commercial court and the obligation to settle his claim at a moderate interest. The National Assembly discussed this issue and made a bill, in the form of a friendly concordat. The Assembly hesitated when it suddenly learned that at that very moment, at the Saint-Denis gate, thousands of wives and children of the insurgents were preparing a petition in favor of amnesty.

Faced with the resurrected specter of June, the petty bourgeois trembled and the Assembly proved implacable. The amicable concordats between creditor and debtor were rejected in their essential points.

After the republican representatives of the bourgeoisie, within the Assembly, had repelled the democratic representatives of the petty bourgeoisie, this parliamentary rupture took on its real bourgeois economic meaning by the fact that the petty bourgeois debtors were handed over to the bourgeois creditors. A large part of the former were completely ruined; as for the others, they were only allowed to continue their trade under conditions that made them dependent serfs of capital. On October 22, 1848, the National Assembly rejected the amicable concordats; on September 19, 1848, in a state of siege, Prince Louis Bonaparte and the detainee of Vincennes, the communist Raspail, were elected representatives of Paris. As for the bourgeoisie, it elected the Jewish banker and Orleanist Fould. Thus, from all sides and at the same time, there was a public declaration of war on the national constituent assembly, on bourgeois republicanism, on Cavaignac.

It is not necessary to explain at length how the mass bankruptcy of the Paris petty bourgeois had repercussions that extended far beyond the circle of those directly affected by it, and how it forcefully shook bourgeois commerce once again. However, the public deficit was further increased by the expenses occasioned by the June insurrection and because state revenues were constantly lowered by the interruption of production, the reduction of consumption, and the restrictions on imports. Cavaignac and the National Assembly could resort to no other means than a new loan that placed them further under the yoke of the financial aristocracy.

If the petty bourgeois had reaped as fruits of the June victory bankruptcy and judicial liquidation, on the other hand, the janissaries of Cavaignac, the gardes mobiles, had their reward in the sweet arms of the harlots, and the "young saviors of society" received tributes of all kinds in the salons of Marrast, the gentleman of the tricolors who represented the double role of host and minstrel of the legal Republic. However, society's preferences for the gardes mobiles and their incomparably higher pay exasperated the army, while all the national illusions that bourgeois republicanism, with its newspaper Le National, had been able to capture under Louis Philippe a portion of the army and the peasant class. The role of mediator played by Cavaignac and the National Assembly in Northern Italy to deliver it to Austria in agreement with England-this single moment of power nullified eighteen years of opposition by the National. No government was less national than that of the National, more dependent on England, while under Louis-Philippe he lived on the daily paraphrase of Cato's motto: Carthaginem esse delendam; no other more servile before the Holy Alliance, while for a Guizot he had asked for the treaties of Vienna to be torn up. The irony of history made Bastide, the former foreign policy editor of the National, the Minister of Foreign Affairs of France, in order that he belied each of his articles with each of his dispatches.

For a moment the army and the peasant class had believed that the military dictatorship would at once put war with the foreigner and "glory" on the French agenda. But Cavaignac was not the dictatorship of the sabre over bourgeois society, he silenced the dictatorship of the bourgeoisie by the sabre. And in matters of soldiering, for the moment the gendarme was enough for him. Cavaignac hid under the severe traces of anti-republican resignation the depressed servility to the humiliating conditions of his bourgeois position. Money has no owner! Like the Constituent Assembly, he idealized this old refrain of the third estate by transposing it into political language: the bourgeoisie has no king, the true form of its domination is the Republic.

To elaborate this form, to make a republican constitution, this is what the "great organic work" of the national constituent assembly consisted of. Changing the names of the Christian calendar to transform it into a republican calendar, exchanging Saint Bartholomew for Saint Robespierre changes the weather or the wind as much as this Constitution modified or was supposed to modify bourgeois society. When it went beyond merely changing customs, it was to legalize already existing facts. This is how it solemnly registered the existence of the Republic, the existence of universal suffrage, the existence of a single sovereign national Assembly instead of two constitutional Chambers with limited powers. This is how she registered and regularized the dictatorship of Cavaignac, replacing the established, unaccountable hereditary royalty with an elective, mobile, accountable legality, a four-year presidency. Thus it even turned into constitutional law the extraordinary powers with which the National Assembly had, as a precaution, equipped its president after the horrors of May 15 and June 25, in the interest of its own security. The rest of the Constitution was a case of terminology. Monarchist labels were torn from the packages of the old royalty, and Republican labels were pasted on. Marrast, the former editor-in-chief of the National, now transformed into editor-in-chief of the Constitution, performed, not without talent, this scholarly task.

The Constituent Assembly looked like that Chilean official who wanted to finish the property reports with the cadastre regulations at the exact moment when the subterranean sounds announced the volcanic eruption that would project the ground beneath his feet into the distance. While in theory it marked on the compass the forms in which the domination of the bourgeoisie was republicanly expressed, in reality it was only maintained by the abolition of all formulas, by force without words, by the state of siege. Two days before beginning its constitutional work, it proclaimed its prolongation. Until then, constitutions were made and adopted as long as the process of social unrest had reached a point of stagnation, as long as the relations formed again between the classes had been consolidated, as long as the rival fractions of the ruling class had reached an agreement that allowed them to continue the struggle among themselves while excluding from it the mass of the weakened people. This Constitution, on the contrary, did not sanction any social revolution, it sanctioned the momentary victory of the old society over the revolution.

In the first draft of the Constitution, written before the days of June, there was still the "right to work", the first clumsy formula where the revolutionary demands of the proletariat were summed up. The right was transformed into assistance: what modern state does not support, in one way or another, its indigents? The right to work is, in the bourgeois sense, a nonsense, a vain desire, worthy of pity; but behind the right to work there is the power over capital, the appropriation of the means of production, its subordination to the associated working class, that is, the suppression of the wage-earner, of capital and its reciprocal relations, Behind the "right to work" there was the June insurrection. This Constituent Assembly, which in effect placed the revolutionary proletarian on the margins of the law, was forced to reject on principle a formula of the Constitution, the law of laws, to cast its anathema on the "right to labor." She didn't stop there. Just as Plato banished the poets from his Republic, she banished the progressive tax from hers forever. Now, the progressive tax is not only a bourgeois measure achievable within the existing relations of production on a more or less broad scale; it is also the only way to bind the middle layers of bourgeois society to the "legal" Republic, to reduce the public debt, and to drive the anti-republican majority of the bourgeoisie to failure.

On the occasion of the friendly concordats, the tricolour

republicans had sacrificed the petty bourgeoisie at will. They elevated this isolated fact to the height of a principle by legally interdicting progressive taxation. They placed bourgeois reform and proletarian revolution on the same plane. But which class was left as the mainstay of this Republic? The big bourgeoisie. And if it exploited the republicans of the National to consolidate the old conditions of economic life, it thought on the other hand of exploiting the strengthened social conditions to restore the political forms that suited it. From the beginning of October, Cavaignac was forced to make Dufaure and Vivien, former ministers of Louis-Filipe, ministers of the Republic, despite the rancor and clamor of the brainless puritans of his own party.

While the tricolored Constitution rejected all compromise with the petty bourgeoisie and could not bring any new element of society into the new State form, it hastened, on the other hand, to bring its traditional inviolability to a point where the old State found its most ardent and fanatical defenders: it raised the irremovability of its judges, questioned by the provisional government, to the level of constitutional law. The king she had dethroned was resurrected by the hundreds into these immovable inquisitors of legality.

The French press had much discussion about the contradictions of Monsieur Marrast's Constitution; for example, the juxtaposition of two sovereigns, the national assembly and the president, etc. etc.

So the main contradiction of this constitution consists in the following: the classes whose social slavery it perpetuated - proletariat, peasants, petty bourgeois - received from it political power with universal suffrage; and from the bourgeoisie, whose former social power it sanctioned, it took away the political guarantees of such power. She narrows her political domination under democratic conditions which at every turn help the enemy classes to gain victory and which call into question the very foundations of bourgeois society. To some, it asks them not to seek their political emancipation until social emancipation; to others, not to abandon social restoration for political restoration.

These contradictions mattered little to the bourgeois republicans. As they ceased to be indispensable (and they were only indispensable as champions of the old society against the revolutionary proletariat), within weeks of their victory they dropped from the level of party to that of "little church. As for the Constitution, they treated it as a great maneuver. What had to be constituted in it was, first of all, the domination of the "little church". The president was to extend in his person the powers of Cavaignac and the legislative assembly was to extend those of the constitution. They hoped to reduce the political power of the masses to an imitation of power, and they thought they could play with this semblance of power sufficiently to raise continually over the heads of the bourgeois majority the dilemma of the June days: either the reign of the National or the reign of anarchy.

The constitutional work that began on September 4 was completed on October 23. On September 2, the Constituent had decided not to dissolve itself until it had promulgated the organic laws that completed the Constitution. However, it decided to put its own creation, the president, into the world as early as December 10, well before the end of its period of activity. In this way she would be sure to greet her mother's son in the homunculus of the Constitution. As a precaution, it was arranged that if none of the candidates obtained two million votes, the election would pass from the nation to the Constituent Assembly.

Useless precautions. The first day the Constitution went into effect was the last day of the Constituent. She was looking for "her mother's son" and found "her uncle's nephew". Saul Cavaignac had been defeated six times.

December 10, 1848 was the day of the peasant revolt. Only on this day dates the February of the French peasants. The symbol that expressed their entry into the revolutionary movement, clumsy and cunning, naive villain, coarse and sublime, a calculated superstition, pathetic burlesque, a genial and stupid anachronism, the trickster of world history, a hieroglyphic indecipherable by reason; it symbolized to the point of confusion the physiognomy of the class that represents barbarism in the bosom of civilization. The Republic had announced itself to this class by the doorman; it announced itself to the Republic by the Emperor. Napoleon was the only man who really represented the interests, and the imagination, of the new peasant class that 1789 had created. By writing her name on the façade of the Republic, she was declaring war on the foreigner and asserting her class interests to the interior. Napoleon was not a man for the peasants, but a program. It was with flags and to the sound of music that they went to the polls, to the cries of "No more taxes, down with the rich, down with the Republic, long live the emperor!" Behind the emperor lurked the jacquerie. The Republic they were defeating with their votes was the Republic of the rich.

December 10 was the coup d'état of the peasants that overthrew the existing government. And from that day on, when they surprised and gave France a government, their eyes were stubbornly fixed on Paris. For a moment active heroes of the revolutionary drama, they could no longer be relegated to the passive and servile role of chorus members.

The other classes contributed to complete the electoral victory of the peasants. Napoleon's election was for the proletariat the ousting of Cavaignac, the fall of the Constituent Assembly, the resignation of the bourgeois republicans. For the petty bourgeoisie, Napoleon was the supremacy of the debtor over the creditor. For the majority of the big bourgeoisie, Napoleon's election was the open rupture with the fraction it had had to serve itself for a time, but which had become unbearable since it had tried to make its momentary position a constitutional one. Napoleon in place of Cavaignac was monarchy in place of the Republic, the beginning of the monarchist restoration, the dOrléans to whom timid allusions were made, the fleur-de-lis hidden beneath the violet. The army, in short, voted for Napoleon against the garde mobile, against the idyll of peace, for war.

This is how it happened, as the Neue Rheinische Zeitung put it, that the simplest man in France acquired the most complex importance. Precisely because he was nothing, he could symbolize everything, except himself. Nevertheless, however different the meaning of Napoleon's name might be on the lips of the different classes, each of them wrote with his name on his ballot: "Down with the party of the National, down with Cavaignac, down with the Constituent, down with the Republic, bourgeois!" Minister Dufaure publicly declared to the Constituent Assembly, "December 10 is a second February 24."

The petty bourgeoisie and the proletariat had voted "en bloc" in favor of Napoleon, in order to vote against Cavaignac and wrest from the Constituent Assembly the final decision to unite their votes. However, the more advanced portion of these two classes presented their own candidates. Napoleon was the common name of tonos the coalition parties against the bourgeois Republic. Ledru-Rollin and Raspail were the natural names, the first of the democratic petty bourgeoisie, the second of the revolutionary proletariat. The votes for Raspail - the proletarians and their spokesmen declared it loud and clear - were to be a simple demonstration: both of protest against any presidency, that is, against the Constitution itself, and of votes against Ledru-Rollin, the first act with which the proletariat detached itself, as an independent political party, from the Democratic Party. This party, on the other hand - the democratic petty bourgeoisie and its parliamentary representation, La Montagne - treated Ledru-Rollin's candidacy with all the seriousness, all the solemnity he used to employ to deceive himself. This was, in fact, his last attempt to impose himself before the proletariat as an independent party. Not only the bourgeois republican party, but the petty bourgeois democratic party and its Montagne, were defeated on December 10.

France now had, next to a Montagne, a Napoleon. Proof that both were but a lifeless caricature of the great realities whose names they bore. Louis-Napoleon with the emperor's hat and the eagle, parodied as miserably the old Napoleon as La Montagne, with his borrowed phrases from 1793 and his demagogic posturing, parodied the old Montagne. Thus, the traditional superstition regarding 1793 was destroyed at the same time as that regarding Napoleon. The revolution only came to have a personality of its own after it had won an original name; and it could only do so after it had brought the modern revolutionary class, the industrial proletariat, imperiously to the fore. One can say that December 10 already disconcerted La Montagne and made him doubt his own sanity, because it broke, by laughing at a mediocre peasant farce, the classical analogy with the old revolution. On December 20, Cavaignac abandoned his duties and the Constituent Assembly proclaimed Louis-Napoleon president of the Republic. On December 19, the last day of its omnipotence, the Assembly rejected the amnesty proposal in favor of the June insurgents. To disapprove the decree of June 27, with which it had condemned fifteen thousand insurrectors to deportation, bypassing the entire judicial sentence, was it not to disapprove of the June battle itself?

Odilon Barrot, the last minister of Louis-Filipe, was the first minister of Louis-Napoleon. Just as Louis Napoleon did not consider December 10 as the day of his power, but rather the senatus consulte of 1806, he found a president of the Council who did not consider December 20 as the date of his ministry, but rather the royal decree of February 24. As the rightful heir of Louis-Philippe, Louis-Napoleon mitigated the change of government by retaining the old ministry, which, incidentally, had not had time to wear out as it had not had time to be born.

The leaders of the bourgeois monarchist fractions advised Louis-Napoleon to take such an attitude. The leadership of the old dynastic opposition, which had unconsciously made the transition towards the republicans of the National, was even more qualified to form, with full consciousness, the transition of the bourgeois republic towards the monarchy.

Odilon Barrot was the leader of the only old opposition party that had not yet worn itself out in the ever vain struggle for a ministerial title. In rapid succession, the revolution projected all the old opposition parties onto the summit of the state, so that they were forced to deny and renege, not only in deed but even in word, on their old formulations, and, gathered together in a disgusting mixture, were finally thrown into the dustbin of history. And no apostasy was spared by this Barrot, this personification of bourgeois liberalism who, for eighteen years, had hidden the miserable emptiness of his spirit behind attitudes of simulated gravity. If, at certain moments, the too shocking contrast between the thorns of the present and the laurels of the past frightened him, a glance in the mirror restored his ministerial posture and a very human admiration for his own person. What was reflected in the mirror was Guizot, whom he had always envied and who had always dominated him, Guizot himself, with Odilon's Olympian forehead. What he couldn't see were the ears of Midas.

The Barrot of February 24 was only revealed in the Barrot of December 20. He, the Orleanist, the Voltairean, chose the Jesuit legitimist Falloux as priest of the cult.

A few days later, the Ministry of the Interior was entrusted to Léon Faucher, a Malthusian economist. Law, religion, political economy! The Barrot ministry contained all of this and was also a union of the legitimists and the Orleanists. They only lacked the Bonapartists, Bonaparte continued to conceal his desire to be Napoleon, for Soulouque did not yet play the role of Les Toussaint Louverture.

As soon as the party of the National left all the high places where it had clung - General Directorate of Police, Directorate of the Post Office, Procurator General, Prefecture of Paris - these posts were all occupied by former creatures of the monarchy.

Changarnier, the legitimist, was given the superior command of the national guard of the Seine department, the garde mobile, and the line troops of the first division. Bugeaud, the Orleanist, was appointed commander-in-chief of the army of the Alps. These changes of officials continued uninterruptedly under Barrot's government. The first act of his ministry was the restoration of the old monarchist administration. In the blink of an eye, the official scene was transformed - backstage, dress, language, actors, extras, cronies, "point," position of the Parties, theme of the drama, content of the conflict, the whole situation. Only the prehistoric Constituent Assembly remained in the same place. But from the moment the National Assembly had installed Bonaparte, from the moment Bonaparte had installed Barrot, from the moment Barrot had installed Changarnier, France was leaving the period of the constitution of the Republic to enter the period of the constituted Republic. And in the constituted Republic what did a constituent assembly have to do? Once the earth was created, the only thing left for its creator to do was to take refuge in heaven, The Constituent Assembly was willing not to follow his example: the National Assembly was the last refuge of the party of bourgeois republicans. If all the commanding posts of executive power had escaped him, did not the constituent omnipotence remain? To hold on at any price to the sovereign post she occupied and from there regain the lost ground was her first thought. Once the Barrot ministry was replaced by a ministry of the National, the royal staff would be forced to leave the administration palace immediately and the tricolor staff would enter there triumphantly. The National Assembly decided to overthrow the ministry, and the ministry itself provided such an occasion for attack that not even the Constituent could imagine anything more opportune.

It is recalled that to the peasants Bonaparte meant "No more taxes!" He had already been installed in his presidential chair for six days when, on the seventh day, December 27, his ministry proposed to maintain the salt tax, the abolition of which the provisional government had decreed. The salt tax shares with the beverage tax the privilege of being the scapegoat of the old French financial system, especially in the eyes of the rural population. The Barrot ministry could not put a more sarcastic epigram for its voters in the mouth of the elected peasants than these words: reinstatement of the salt tax! With the salt tax, Bonaparte lost his revolutionary salt, the Napoleon of peasant insurrection dissipated like a cloud, and only the great unknown of bourgeois monarchist intrigue remained. And it was not without intention that the Barrot ministry made this act of gross and brutal disillusionment the first governmental act of the president.

For its part, the Constituent eagerly seized the double opportunity of overthrowing the ministry and imposing itself before the peasants' elected representatives as the defender of the peasants' interests. It rejected the Finance Minister's proposal, reduced the tax on salt to one third of its former amount, thus increasing by sixty million a public deficit of five hundred and sixty million, and quietly waited after this vote of no confidence for the withdrawal of the ministry. How little she understood the new world around her and the change that had come over her own position! Behind the ministry was the president, and behind the president were six million citizens who had cast in the ballot box an equal number of votes of no confidence in the Constituent Assembly. The Constituent would return to the nation its vote of no confidence. Ridiculous exchange! She had forgotten that her votes had lost their value. The rejection of the salt tax only matured the decision of Bonaparte and his ministry "to do away" with the Constituent Assembly. The long duel that took up a whole half of the Constituent Assembly's existence began. January 29, March 21 and May 3 are the days, the great days of this crisis, true preliminaries to June 13.

The French, Louis Blanc for example, saw January 29th as the emergence of a constitutional contradiction, the contradiction between a sovereign, indissoluble National Assembly, born of universal suffrage, and a President responsible for it, according to law, but who in reality had not only been equally sanctioned by universal suffrage, and therefore gathered about his person all the voices that had been distributed and dispersed hundreds of times over the different members of the National Assembly, but was also in full possession of all the executive power over which the National Assembly hovers only by way of moral force. This interpretation of June 29 confuses the language of the struggle on the tribune, by the press, in the political associations, with its actual content. Louis Bonaparte facing the constituent National Assembly was not one side of the constitutional power facing the other, it was not the executive power facing the legislative power; it was the constituted bourgeois republic itself in the face of the ambitious intrigues and ideological claims of the revolutionary bourgeois fraction which had founded it and which, astonished, now sought to make the constituted republic resemble a restored monarchy and which wanted to maintain by violence the constituent period with its conditions, its illusions, its language and its personnel, and to prevent the maturing bourgeois republic from appearing in its finished and particular form. Just as the national constituent Assembly represented Cavaignac back in its bosom, Bonaparte represented the national legislative Assembly that had not yet separated from him, that is, the national Assembly of the constituted bourgeois Republic.

The election of Bonaparte could not be explained without putting in the place of a single name its multiple meanings, without seeing its repetition in the election of the new national Assembly. December 10 had annulled the mandate of the old Assembly. On January 29, therefore, it was not the president and the National Assembly of the same Republic that confronted each other, but the National Assembly of the potential Republic and the de facto president of the Republic, two forces that embodied two very different periods in the process of the Republic's existence; It was the small republican fraction of the bourgeoisie that could only proclaim the Republic, wrest it from the revolutionary proletariat through street battles and terror, and sketch in the constitution the fundamental traits of its ideal; and, on the other hand, the whole monarchist multitude of the bourgeoisie, that could only reign in this bourgeois constituted Republic, bring its ideological accessories to the constitution, and realize, with its legislation and its administration, the conditions indispensable to the enslavement of the proletariat.

The storm that fell on January 29 had been brewing throughout that month. The Constituent wanted, with its vote of no confidence, to make the Barrot Ministry resign. The Barrot Ministry, on the contrary, proposed to the Constituent Assembly that it grant itself a definitive vote of no confidence, that it decide on its own suicide, that it decree its own dissolution. Rateau, one of the most obscure deputies, made the proposal to the Constituent on the order of the ministry, on January 6, to this same Constituent which, since August, had decided not to dissolve itself until it had promulgated a whole series of organic laws completing the Constitution. The Fould ministry frankly declared to her that the dissolution was necessary "to restore her shaken credit." Had she not shaken that credit by prolonging the provisional state, by calling into question again with Barrot, Bonaparte, and, with Bonaparte, the constituted Republic? Barrot, the Olympian, transformed into Orlando Furioso, faced with the prospect of having the cabinet presidency torn from him again, after having enjoyed it only a fortnight, and which the Republicans had already extended once in a decade of ten months, Barrot triumphed in tyranny over the tyrant with regard to this miserable Assembly. The mildest of his words were, "For her, there is no possible future." And, in reality, she represented nothing but the past. "She is incapable of surrounding the Republic with the institutions necessary for its consolidation," he added, ironically. Indeed! At the same time that, by her exclusive opposition to the proletariat, her bourgeois energy had been compromised, by her opposition to the monarchists her republican exaltation had been strengthened. She was thus doubly incapable of consolidating by adequate institutions the bourgeois Republic she no longer understood.

With Rateau's proposal, the ministry provoked at the same time a storm of petitions throughout the country, and daily, from all corners of France, the Constituent received in her face veritable bundles of "love letters" in which it was begged, more or less categorically, that she dissolve herself and make her will. In turn, the Constituent was provoked against petitions in which she was urged to continue living. The electoral struggle between Bonaparte and Cavaignac was repeated in the form of a struggle of petitions for or against the dissolution of the national Assembly. The petitions would become the December 10 comments made later. This agitation persisted throughout the month of January.

In the conflict between the Constituent Assembly and the President, the Constituent Assembly could not go back to the general elections as its origin, because someone would remind it of universal suffrage. It could not rely on any regular power, because it was a struggle against legal power. She could not overthrow the ministry with the votes of no confidence, as she had tried again on January 6 and 26, because the ministry did not ask for her confidence. There was only one possibility left to him, insurrection.

The armed forces of the insurrection were the republican party of the national guard, the garde mobile, and the centers of the revolutionary proletariat, the political associations. The gardes mobites, those heroes of the June days, constituted in December the organized armed forces of the republican fractions of the bourgeoisie, just as, before June, the national workshops had formed the organized armed forces of the revolutionary proletariat. In the same way that the executive committee of the Constituent Assembly concentrated its brutality on attacking the national workshops when it needed to put an end to the unbearable demands of the proletariat, so too Bonaparte's ministry fought the garde mobile when it needed to put an end to the unbearable demands of the republican fractions of the bourgeoisie.

And he ordered the dissolution of the garde mobile. The other half received, in place of their democratic organization, a monarchist organization, and their pay was lowered to the level of the common pay of the line troops. The garde mobile found itself in the situation of the June insurrectionists, and every day the press issued public confessions in which the guard acknowledged its June error and begged the proletariat to forgive it.

And the political associations? From the moment the Assembly put into question, in the person of Barrot, the President; and, in the President, the constituted bourgeois Republic; and, in the bourgeois Republic in general, all the constitutive elements of the February Republic; from that moment on, all the parties that wished to overthrow the existing Republic, and that wished to transform it by a process of violent regression into the Republic of their interests and of their class concepts, profiled themselves around it. But what had been done was yet again to be done, the crystallization of the revolutionary movement was again grounded, the Republic that was being fought for was once again the vague Republic of the February days that each party reserved to define itself. The parties briefly resumed their old February positions, but without sharing their illusions. The tricolor Republicans of the National supported themselves again with the Democratic Republicans of La Réforme and put them in the vanguard, at the forefront of the parliamentary struggle. The Democratic Republicans have leaned again on the Socialist Republicans - on January 27, a public manifesto proclaimed their reconciliation and union - and they are preparing in the political associations their second insurrectionary plan. The ministerial press rightly treated the tricolor Republicans of the National as resurrected insurgents of June. To keep themselves at the head of the bourgeois Republic, they have called that very Republic into question. On January 26, Minister Faucher proposed a bill on the right of association whose first paragraph was conceived thus: "Political associations are prohibited." He proposed that this bill be put up for discussion immediately, under the urgency procedure. The Constituent rejected the urgency proposal, and on January 27, Ledru-Rollln submitted a proposal to put the ministry on trial for violating the Constitution, a proposal that had two hundred and thirty signatures. The indictment ofthe ministry at the moment when such an act revealed the awkward confession ofthe impotence ofthe judge, that is, ofthe majority ofthe Chamber, or even the impotent protest ofthe accuser against this very majority, such was the great revolutionary trump card that La Montagne, the younger sister, played immediately at each height ofthe crisis. Poor Montagne, crushed under the weight ofher own name!

On May 15, Blanqui, Barbes, Raspail, etc. had attempted to dissolve the Constituent Assembly by force, penetrating the session hall in front of the Parisian proletariat. Barrot prepared a moral May 15 for this Assembly, wanting to dictate to it its own dissolution and close its session room. The Assembly had charged Barrot with the inquiry into the May accused; and it was at the moment when he appeared before it as a monarchist Blanqui, when it sought before it allies in the political associations, with the revolutionary proletariats, in the party of Blanqui, that the inexorable Barrot tortured it with his proposal to rob the jury of the May accused and summon them before the supreme court invented by the party ofthe National, before the High Court. What a remarkable thing that the tenacious fear of losing a ministerial title could extract from Barrot's head ironies worthy of a Beaumarchais! After long hesitations, the National Assembly adopted his proposal. Faced with the accused of the May bombing, it had returned to its normal character.

If the Constituent, before the president and the ministers, was obliged to insurrection, the president and the ministry, before the Constituent, were obliged to the coup d'état, because they did not have any legal means to dissolve it. But the Constituent was the mother ofthe Constitution, and the Constitution was the mother of the president. With the coup d'état, the president would tear up the Constitution and destroy his republican titles.

He was then forced to show his imperial titles, but his imperial titles evoked the Orleanist titles, and both pale in the face of the legitimist titles. The overthrow of the legal Republic could only bring about its extreme antipode, the legitimist monarchy, at the moment when the Orleanist party was still only the loser of February, when Bonaparte was still only the winner of December 10, and when neither of them could yet oppose the republican usurpation other than their equally usurped monarchist titles. The legitimists were aware that the moment was favorable; they conspired in broad daylight. With General Cavaignac, they could hope to find their Monk. The advent of the white monarchy was proclaimed as openly in their political associations as the advent of the red republic in the proletarian political associations.

By a rebellion fortunately suppressed, the ministry would have rid itself of all difficulties. "Legality kills us" cried Odilon Barrot. A rebellion would have allowed, under the pretext of public safety, to dissolve the Constituent, to violate the Constitution in the interest of the Constitution itself. Odilon Barrot's brutal intervention in the National Assembly, the proposed dissolution of the political associations, the rumored dismissal of fifty tricolor mayors and their replacement by monarchists, the dissolution of the garde mobile, the brutal way in which Changarnier treated his commanders, the reinstatement of Lherminier, that teacher already impossible under Guizot, the toleration of legitimist braggadocio, were also incitements to rebellion. But the rebellion remained deaf. It was waiting for the signal from the Constituent, not from the ministry.

Finally, January 29 arrived, the day on which the pronouncement on Mathieu's (de la Drôme) proposal would take place, aiming at the unconditional rejection of Rateau's proposal. Legitimists, Orleanists, Bonapartists, garde mobile, La Montagne, political associations, everyone was conspiring that day, as much against the alleged enemy as against the considered ally. Bonaparte, on horseback, was reviewing part of the troops in the Place de la Concorde; Changarnier was strutting about in a great display of strategic maneuvers. The Constituent Assembly found its session room militarily occupied. It, the center where all the hopes, beliefs, expectations, fermentations, tensions, and conjurations intersected, the Assembly with lion's courage did not hesitate a moment longer when it came closer than ever to the moment to surrender its soul. She looked like that fighter who feared not only to use her own weapons, but believed equally in the duty to keep her opponent's weapons intact. Despising death, she signed her death warrant and rejected Rateau's unconditional rejection. She herself in a state of siege imposed limits on her constituent activity whose necessary framework had been the state of siege of Paris. She took her revenge in a dignified way by deciding, the next day, to hold an inquiry into the fright the ministry had caused her on January 29. La Montagne gave proof of her lack of revolutionary energy and political sense by letting the party of the National make her the herald of the armed forces in that comedy of intrigue. This party had made a last attempt to maintain once again, in the constituted Republic, the monopoly of power that it had possessed during the period of formation of the bourgeois Republic. This attempt failed.

If the January crisis was about the existence of the Constituent, the March 21 crisis was about the existence of the Constitution. No longer is the personnel of the national party at issue this time, but its ideal.

We need not mention that the Republicans made their lofty sentiment of their ideology pay less dearly than the earthly enjoyment of governmental power.

On March 21, the agenda of the National Assembly included Faucher's bill against the right of association: the prohibition of political associations. Article eight of the Constitution guaranteed all French people the right of association. The prohibition of political associations was then an absolutely clear attack on the Constitution; and the Constituent should itself canonize the desecration of its saints. But political associations were the rallying points, the places of conspiracy of the revolutionary proletariat. The National Assembly itself had forbidden the coalition of the workers against their bourgeois. And were political associations anything other than the coalition of the entire working class against the entire bourgeois class, the formation of a workers' state against the bourgeois state? Were they not so much constituent assemblies of the proletariat as detachments to the ranks of the army of revolt? What the Constituent was to constitute, first of all, was the domination of the bourgeoisie. The Constitution could not, then, manifestly understand by right of association anything other than associations in agreement with the domination of the bourgeoisie, that is, with bourgeois order. If, for theoretical convenience, it expressed itself in a general way, wasn't the Government there, as well as the national Assembly, to interpret and apply it in particular cases? And if, in the antediluvian epoch of the Republic, political associations were prohibited de facto by the state of siege, was it not necessary to prohibit them by law in the regular, constituted Republic? The tricolored republicans had only one redundant formula of the Constitution to oppose this prosaic interpretation of the Constitution. One portion of them, Pagnerre, Duclerc, etc., voted for the ministry, thus giving it a majority. The other portion, Archangel Cavaignac and Church Father Marrast at the head, withdrew when the article on the prohibition of political associations passed to a special commission and, with Ledru-Rollin and La Montagne, "gathered council." The National Assembly was paralyzed, it no longer had a quorum. Monsieur Crémieux, in the cabinet, remembered in time that this cabinet led straight into the street and that it was no longer February 1848, but March 1849. Suddenly enlightened, the party of the National reentered the session room of the National Assembly. It was followed by La Montagne once more deceived, who, constantly tormented by revolutionary yearnings, was also constantly looking for constitutional possibilities and always felt better in her place behind the bourgeois republicans than in front of the revolutionary proletariat. The comedy was staged. And it had been the Constituent, the very Constituent, who had decreed that violation of the letter of the Constitution was the only accomplishment in keeping with its spirit.

Only one point remained to be settled: the relations of the constituted Republic with the European revolution, its foreign policy. On May 8, 1849, unrest raged in the Constituent Assembly, whose mandate was to expire in a few days. The attack of the French army on Rome, its retreat before the Romans, its political infamy and military disgrace, the assassination of the Roman Republic by the French Republic, the first campaign of the second Bonaparte's Italy, were on the agenda. La Montagne had once more played his great trump card; Ledru-Rollin had laid on the President's desk the inevitable act of indictment against the ministry for violation of the Constitution, and this time also against Bonaparte.

The May 8 scenario was repeated later, on June 13. Let's explain about the Roman expedition.

As early as mid-November 1848, Cavaignac had sent a battle fleet to Civita-Vecchia to protect the pope, put him on board, and drive him to France. The pope was to bless the legal Republic and secure Cavaignac's election to the presidency. With the pope, Cavaignac wanted to attract the priests, with the priests the peasants, and with the peasants the presidency. Electoral propaganda in its immediate aim, Cavaignac's expedition was both a protest and a threat against the Roman revolution. It was the germ of France's intervention in favor of the pope.

This intervention in favor of the pope, with Austria and Naples, against the Roman Republic, was decided at the first session of Bonaparte's Council of Ministers on December 23. Falloux in the ministry was the pope in Rome and the pope's Rome. Bonaparte no longer needed the pope to be president of the peasants, but he needed the pope to keep the peasants from the president. It was the credulity of the peasants that made him a president. With the faith they lost their credulity, and with the pope, their faith. And the coalitioned Orleanists and legitimists who reigned in

Bonaparte's name! Before restoring the king, it was necessary to restore the power that consecrates kings. Abstraction made of his monarchism: without the old Rome submissive to his temporal power, no pope; without the pope, no Catholicism, no French religion; and without religion what would become of the old French society? The mortgage that the peasant holds on heavenly goods guarantees the mortgage that the bourgeois holds on the peasant's goods. The Roman revolution was, then, an attack against property, against the bourgeois order, as terrible as the June revolution. The bourgeois domination restored in France required the restoration of pontifical domination in Rome. Finally, the Roman revolutionaries were fighting the allies of the French revolutionaries. The alliance of the counter-revolutionary classes in the constituted French Republic had its necessary complement in the alliance of that Republic with the Holy Alliance, with Naples and Austria. The decision of the Council of Ministers of December 23 was no secret to the Constituent Assembly. Already on January 8 Ledru-Rollin had questioned the cabinet on this matter. The ministry denied it, the National Assembly moved to the agenda. Did she trust the ministry's words? We know that she spent the whole month of January granting him votes of no confidence. But if he was in his role of lying, she was in her role of pretending to believe his lies and thus saving republican appearances.

However, Piedmont was defeated. Charles-Albert abdicated. The Austrian army was knocking on the gates of France. Ledru-Rollin made a violent intervention. The ministry proved that it only continued in Northern Italy the policy of Cavaignac, and Cavaignac the policy of the provisional government, that is, of Ledru-Rollin. Moreover, this time he reaped a vote of confidence from the National Assembly and was authorized to temporarily occupy a suitable seat in Upper Italy to thus assist the peaceful negotiations with Austria on the integrity of Sardinian territory and on the Roman question. As is well known, the fate of Italy is decided on the battlefields of Northern Italy. This was why Rome had fallen with Lombardy and Piedmont; or else it was necessary for France to declare war on Austria and, as a consequence, on the European counter-revolution. Was the National Constituent Assembly suddenly taking over the Barrot Ministry for the Committee of Public Safety, or was it itself taking over the Convention? Why then the military occupation of a point in Upper Italy? The expedition against Rome was hidden under this transparent veil.

On April 14, fourteen thousand men, under Oudinot's command, sailed toward Civita-Vecchia. On April 16, the National Assembly granted the ministry a credit of one million two hundred thousand francs for the conservation, for three months, of an intervention fleet in the Mediterranean. It thus gave the ministry all the means to intervene against Rome, while pretending to make it intervene against Austria. She didn't see what the ministry was doing, she didn't hear what it was saying. One could not find such faith in Israel: the Constituent had come to not know what the Constituent Republic should do.

Finally, on May 8, the last scene of the comedy was played. The Constituent Assembly invited the Ministry to take swift measures to bring the expedition from Italy back to the objective that had been set for it. Bonaparte that same afternoon inserted a letter in the Moniteur in which he addressed his heartiest congratulations to Oudinot. On May 11, the Assembly repelled the act of accusation against this same Bonaparte and his ministry. And La Montagne, who, instead of breaking through this web of lies, took the parliamentary comedy seriously in order to play herself the role of Fouquier-Tinville, did not let the lion skin borrowed from the Convention show the petty-bourgeois calf skin which was natural to her!

The second half of the Constituent's existence is summarized thus: it recognizes, on January 29, that the bourgeois monarchist fractions are the natural leaders of the Republic constituted by it; on March 21, that the violation of the Constitution is its realization; and, on May 11, that the emphatically proclaimed passive alliance of the French Republic with the peoples in struggle means its active alliance with the European counter-revolution, This miserable Assembly left the scene after having given itself, two days before its birth anniversary, on May 4, the satisfaction of rejecting the amnesty proposal in favor of the June insurgents. With her power shattered, hated to death by the people, repelled, mistreated, dismissed with disdain by the bourgeoisie of which she was the instrument, constrained in the second half of her existence to renege on the first, deprived of her republican illusion, without great achievements in the past, without hope for the future, a living body decaying to pieces, she did not know how to revive her own corpse except by constantly recalling the June victory, reliving it afterwards; she sustained herself by cursing the damned again and again. Vampire living off the blood of the June insurgents.

She left behind her the public deficit increased by the expenses of the June insurrection, the suppression of the salt tax, the indemnities granted to the planters with the abolition of slavery, the expenses of the Roman expedition, and the suppression of the liquor tax, whose abolition she decided on already in her last gasps; old lady with malignant glee, happy to place on the shoulders of her satisfied heir a compromising debt of honor.

Since the beginning of March, electoral unrest had begun in favor of the National Legislative Assembly. Two main groups were confronting each other: the Party of Order and the Democratic-Socialist or Red Party. Among them were the Friends of the Constitution, in the name of which the tricolor Republicans of the National were trying to represent a party. The party of order was formed immediately after the June days; it was only after December 10 had allowed it to push aside the "little church" of the National, the bourgeois republicans, that the secret of its existence, the coalition of Orleanists and legitimists into one party, was revealed. The bourgeois class was divided into two great fractions which, one at a time - the large landed property under the Restoration, the financial aristocracy, and the industrial bourgeoisie under the July monarchy - had held the monopoly of power. Bourbon was the royal name covering the preponderant influence of the interests of one of the fractions. Orléans was the one covering the preponderant influence of the interests of the other fraction: the anonymous reign of the Republic was the only yoke under which the two fractions could maintain with legal power their common class interests without renouncing their reciprocal rivalry. If the bourgeois Republic could be nothing other than the finished, perfectly clear domination of the entire bourgeois class, could it be anything other than the domination of the Orleanists completed by the legitimists and the legitimists completed by the Orleanists, the synthesis of Restoration and July monarchy? The bourgeois republicans of the National did not represent a large fraction of their class from an economic point of view. They had as their only importance and as their only historical title the fact that, under the monarchy, before the two bourgeois fractions who only understood their particular regime, they had enforced the general regime of the bourgeois class, the anonymous regime of the Republic which they idealized and decorated with ancient arabesques, but where they saluted above all the domination of their group. If the party of the National doubted its own lucidity when it realized at the summit of the Republic that it had created the coalition monarchists, these were no less mistaken themselves about their unified domination. They did not understand that if any of their fractions considered apart were monarchists, the result of their chemical combination must necessarily be republican, and that the white monarchy and the blue monarchy must necessarily neutralize each other in the tricolor republic. Forced, by their opposition to the revolutionary proletariat and the intermediate classes that grouped more and more around them, to recruit their combined forces, each of the fractions of the party of order, faced with the other's desires for restoration and hegemony, was driven to make the common domination prevail, that is, the republican form of bourgeois domination. Thus, those monarchists who at first believed in an immediate restoration, and who later, while preserving the republican form, foamed mortal invectives against it, behold, they finally recognized that they could not agree on anything but the Republic, and postponed the Restoration to an indeterminate date. The common lust for power strengthened each of the two fractions and made them even more incapable and less willing to subordinate themselves to the other, or rather, to restore the monarchy.

The party of order directly proclaimed in its electoral program the domination of the bourgeois class, that is, the maintenance of the conditions of existence of its domination, of property, of the family, of religion, of order! It naturally presented its class domination and the conditions of its class domination as the necessary conditions of material production, as well as the ensuing social relations. The Party of Order had enormous resources. It organized its branches throughout France; it had at its disposal all the ideologues of the old society, it had the influence of the existing governmental power; it possessed an army of spontaneous vassals throughout the mass of petty bourgeois and peasants who, still estranged from the revolutionary movement, saw in the great dignitaries of property the natural representatives of their small property and petty prejudices; represented throughout the country by a multitude of kings, he could punish the repudiation of his candidates as an insurrection, dismiss the rebellious workers, the agricultural and domestic laborers, the petty officials, the railway employees, the recalcitrant bureaucrats, all the officials who were bourgeoisly subordinate to him. He could, in short, by this and that, maintain the illusion that the republican Constituent Assembly had prevented the Bonaparte of December 10 from manifesting his miraculous forces. In the party of order, we do not mention the Bonapartists. They were not a serious fraction of the bourgeois class, but a heap of old invalids and superstitious, and young, unbelieving gentlemen of industry. The party of order triumphed in the elections and sent a large majority to the legislative assembly.

In the face of the coalitioned counterrevolutionary bourgeois class, the already revolutionary partics of the petty bourgeoisie and the peasant class would naturally have to link up with the great dignitary of revolutionary interests, the revolutionary proletariat. We have seen that the democratic spokesmen of the petty bourgeoisie in Parliament, that is, La Montagne, had been thrown by parliamentary defeats towards the socialist spokesmen of the proletariat, and that the real petty bourgeoisie outside Parliament had been thrown towards the real proletarians by friendly concordats, by the preponderance of bourgeois interests, by bankruptcy. On January 27, La Montagne and the socialists had celebrated their reconciliation; they renewed, at the great banquet of February 1849, their pact of alliance. The social party and the democratic party, the party of the workers and the party of the petty bourgeoisie, united in the Social-Democratic Party, that is, the Red Party.

Paralyzed for a few moments by the agony that followed the June days, the French Republic, after the suspension of the state of siege, after October 14, had gone through a continuous series of feverish emotions. First of all, the struggle for the presidency; then; the struggle of the president against the Constituent; the struggle for the political associations; the Bourges process, which, in the face of the petty figures of the president, the coalition monarchists, the legal republicans, the democratic La Montagne, the socialist doctrinaires of the proletariat, made the real revolutionaries of this same proletariat appear like antediluvian monsters left on the surface of society by a deluge, or even as if, alone, they could precede a social deluge; the electoral agitation; the execution of the assassins of Bréa, the continuous attacks of the press, the violent police raids of the Government on the banquets the impudent monarchist provocations; the exposure of the figures of Louis Blanc and Gaussidiêre to public execration; the uninterrupted struggle between the constituted Republic and the Constituent, which made, at every instant, the revolution return to its starting point, which made, at every instant, the victor the vanquished, the vanquished the victor, which, in the twinkling of an eye, threw to the ground the position of the parties and classes, their separations and their connections; the rapid march of the European counter-revolution; the glorious struggle of Hungary, the conscription of the German defenses, the Roman expedition, the shameful defeat of the French army at Rome: in this whirlwind, in this painful historical disorder, in this dramatic ebb and flow of passions, of hopes, of revolutionary disillusions, the various classes of French society would necessarily have to count in weeks their periods of development, just as in other times they counted them by half centuries. An important part of the peasants and the provinces were in revolution. Not only had Napoleon disappointed them, but the Red Party had offered them content instead of name, instead of the illusory exemption from taxation, the reimbursement of the billions paid to the legitimists, the regulation of mortgages and the suppression of usury.

The army itself was contaminated by revolutionary fever. By voting for Bonaparte, it had voted for victory and he gave it defeat; it had voted for the corporal behind whom the great revolutionary captain hides, and he gave it back the great generals behind whom the corporal expert in gaiter buttons is concealed. There is no doubt that the Red Party, that is, the coalition Democratic Party, in the absence of victory, thought to celebrate at least the great triumph that Paris, the army, a respectable portion of the provinces would vote for him. Ledru-Rollín, the leader of La Montagne, was elected by five departments. None of the leaders of the party of order achieved such a victory. No name from the proletarian party proper. This election reveals to us the secret of the Democratic-Socialist Party. If La Montagne, the parliamentary vanguard of the petty bourgeoisie democrats, was, on the one hand, forced to unite with the socialist doctrinaires of the proletariat, the latter, forced by the formidable material defeat of June to get back on its feet through intellectual victories, not being yet in a position, in view of the development of the other classes, to seize the revolutionary dictatorship, was obliged to throw itself into the arms of the doctrinaires of its emancipation, of the founders of socialist sects; on the other hand, the revolutionary peasants, the army, the provinces stood behind La Montagne, who thus became the leader of the revolutionary army camp, and, by his agreement with the socialists, had removed all antagonism in the revolutionary party. In the last half of the Constitution's existence, La Montagne, in it, represented the republican pathos, and had made him forget his sins of the time of the Provisional Government, the Executive Committee, and the June days. As the party of the National, according to its indecisive nature, allowed itself to be crushed by the monarchist ministry, the party of La Montagne, pushed aside during the omnipotence of the National, grew and prevailed as the parliamentary representative of the Revolution. In effect, the party of the National had nothing to oppose the monarchist fractions except ambitious personalities and idealistic platitudes. La Montagne's party, on the contrary, represented a floating mass between the bourgeoisie and the proletariat whose material interests demanded democratic institutions. Faced with the Cavaignacs and the Marrasts, Ledru-Rollín and La Montagne were consequently in the truth of the revolution, and drew from the consciousness of this grave situation an even greater courage, since the manifestation of revolutionary energy was limited to parliamentary departures, the handing down of acts of accusation, threats, outbursts of voices, tonite speeches, and extremisms which did not go beyond the level of words. The peasants were almost in the same situation as the petty bourgeois; they had almost the same social demands to make. All the middle layers of society, as they were exercised in the revolutionary movement, would necessarily find their hero in Ledru-Rollin. He was the character of the democratic petty bourgeoisie. Faced with the party of order, it was precisely the reformers of that order, half conservative, half revolutionary and absolutely utopian, who were first and foremost to be thrown to the front.

National's party, the "friends of the Constitution itself,"

"the pure and simple Republicans," were soundly defeated in the elections. A tiny minority among them was sent to the legislative chamber. Their most notorious leaders disappeared from the scene, even Marrast, the editor-in-chief, the Orpheus of the legal Republic.

On May 28, the legislative assembly met; on June 11, the shock of May 8 was repeated. Ledru-Rollin placed, on behalf of La Montagne, a request for an indictment against the president and the ministry for violation of the Constitution because of the attack on Rome. On June 12, the legislative assembly rejected the request for indictment, just as the constituent assembly had rejected it on May 11; but this time the proletariat sent La Montagne into the street, not, however, for street combat, but for street demonstration. Suffice it to say that La Montagne was at the head of this movement for it to be known that the movement was defeated and that June 1849 was a caricature, as ridiculous as it was undignified, of June 1848. The great retreat of June 13 was only not eclipsed by the even greater account of the battle by Changarnier, the great man who improvised the party of order. Every social moment needs its great men; and if it does not find them, it invents them, as Helvetius said.

On December 20, there was only half of the constituted bourgeois republic, the president; on May 29, it was completed by the other half, the legislative Assembly, In June 1848, the constituting bourgeois republic had etched its birth in the annals of history with an unspeakable battle against the proletariat; in June 1849, the constituted bourgeois republic did the same, but with an unspeakable comedy played out with the bourgeoisie. June 1849 was the Nemesis of June 1848. In June 1849, it was not the workers who were the losers, but the petty bourgeois placed between them and the revolution were the losers. June 1849 was not the bloody tragedy between wage labor and capital, but the spectacle rich in scenes of arrests, the pitiful spectacle between the debtor and the creditor. The party of order had won, it was the almighty, it now needed to show who it was.

CHAPTER III: JUNE 13, 1849 - MARCH 10, 1850

On December 20, the Janus head of the constitutional Republic had only shown one of its faces, the executive face, under the indecisive and inexpressive strokes of Louis Bonaparte: on May 29, 1849, it showed its second face, the legislative, creased with wrinkles left by the orgies of the Restoration and the July monarchy. With the National Legislative Assembly, the constitutional Republic appeared, ready, under its static republican form in which the domination of the bourgeois class is constituted, the common domination of the two great monarchist fractions that form the French bourgeoisie, the legitimists and the coalitionist Orleanists, the party of order. While the French Republic was thus becoming the property of the coalition of monarchist parties, the European coalition of counter-revolutionary powers was undertaking, in the same movement, a general crusade against the last refuges of the March revolutions. Russia was violently invading Hungary, Prussia was marching against the constitutional army of the Empire, and Oudinot was attacking Rome. The European crisis was manifestly approaching a decisive turn. The eyes of all Europe were fixed on Paris, the eyes of all Paris on the Legislative Assembly.

On June 11, Ledru-Rollin rose to the rostrum, made no speech, and formulated a requisition against the ministers, naked, without apparatus, based on the facts, concentrated, violent.

The attack against Rome is an attack against the Constitution, the attack against the Roman Republic, an attack against the French Republic. Article five of the Constitution says: "The French Republic never employs its forces against the liberty of any people," and the President directs the French army against Roman liberty. Article fifty-four of the Constitution forbids the executive power to declare any war without the consent of the national assembly. The decision of the Constituent Assembly of May 8 expressly orders the ministers to bring the Roman expedition back to its original determination as soon as possible; it then also expressly forbids war against Rome - and Oudinott attacks Rome. Thus Ledru-Rollin summoned the Constitution itself as a prosecution witness against Bonaparte and his ministers. The monarchist measure of the National Assembly he threw in its face, he, the tribune of the Constitution, this threatening declaration: "The republicans will know how to enforce the Constitution by all means, even by force of arms!" "By force of arms!" repeated the echo of a hundred voices from La Montagne. The majority responded with a terrible uproar. The president of the National Assembly called Ledru-Rollin to order. Ledru-Rollin repeated his provocative statement and finally laid on the table the proposed indictment of Bonaparte and his ministers. The National Assembly, by three hundred and sixty-one votes against two hundred and three, decided, with regard to the attack on Rome, to simply move on to the order of the day.

Ledru-Rollin believed he could defeat the national assembly with the constitution and the president with the national assembly?

The Constitution forbade, it is true, any attack against the freedom of foreign countries, but what the French army was attacking in Rome was not, according to the ministry, "freedom" but the "despotism of anarchy". Despite all his experiences in the

Constituent Assembly, La Montagne had not yet understood that the interpretation of the Constitution belonged only to those who had caused it to be accepted? That it was necessary that its text be interpreted in its viable sense, and that the bourgeois sense was its only viable sense? That Bonaparte and the monarchist majority of the National Assembly were the authentic interpreters of the Constitution, as the priest is the authentic interpreter of the Bible, and the judge the authentic interpreter of the Law? Was the national Assembly fresh from the general election going to allow itself to be chained by the testamentary provisions of the dead Constituent, whose will an Odilon Barrot had torn to pieces in mid-life? Referring to the decision of the Constituent of May 8, had Ledru-Rollín forgotten that this same Constituent had on May 11 rejected his first proposal to indict Bonaparte and his ministers, that it had acquitted the President and the ministers, that it had thus sanctioned as "constitutional" the attack against Rome, that it only made an appeal against a judgment already made, and that it, finally, called the monarchist Legislative a republican Constituent? The Constitution itself appealed to the insurrection by calling, in a special article, for every citizen to defend it. Ledru-Rollin relied on this article. But aren't the public powers equally organized to protect the Constitution, and doesn't the violation of the Constitution begin only from the moment one of the constitutional public powers rebels against the other? And the president of the Republic, the ministers of the Republic, the national Assembly of the Republic were in the most harmonious agreement.

What La Montagne was seeking, on June 11, was an "insurrection at the limits of pure reason," that is, a purely parliamentary insurrection. Intimidated by the prospect of an armed rebellion of the masses of the people, the majority of the Assembly had to break down, in Bonaparte and his ministers, its own power and the meaning of its own election. Had not the Constituent sought in a similar way to annul Bonaparte's election when it insisted so ardently on the removal of the Barrot-Falloux ministry?

Examples of parliamentary insurrections in Convention times were not lacking, when the relations of majority to minority had been broken down at one blow, from top to bottom - and why should the young Montagne not have been able to do what the old one had accomplished? The conditions of the moment did not seem unfavorable to such an enterprise. Social unrest had reached a disturbing degree in Paris, the army no longer seemed, according to its votes, to be very inclined to the Government, the legislative majority was still too recent, too recent to consolidate, and, moreover, it was composed of old people. If La Montagne succeeded in a parliamentary insurrection, the helm of the State would immediately be in his hands. For its part, the democratic petty bourgeoisie, as always, wanted nothing more impatiently than to see the fight begin above its head, in the clouds, among the spirits of the dead in Parliament. Finally, both, the petty bourgeoisie democrats and their representative, La Montagne, with a parliamentary insurrection, realized their great objective: to break the power of the bourgeoisie without removing the chains of the proletariat, or without doing it in any other way than in perspective; the proletariat would be used without it becoming dangerous.

After the June 11 vote of the National Assembly, an interview between some members of La Montagne and delegates from workers' secret societies took place. The delegates insisted that a movement be started that very night. La Montagne resolutely rejected this plan. She did not want, under any price, to let the helm be taken out of her hands; her allies were as suspicious to her as her opponents, and rightly so. The memory of June 1848 stirred more vividly than ever the ranks of the Parisian proletariat. The latter, however, was bound by its alliance with La Montagne. It represented the largest party in the departments, it abused its influence in the army, it had the democratic part of the national guard, it had behind it the moral power of commerce. To begin the insurrection at this moment, against her will, was for the proletariat, decimated moreover by cholera, expelled en masse from Paris by unemployment, to uselessly repeat the days of June 1848 without the conditions they had imposed on that desperate struggle. The proletarian delegates did the only rational thing: they got a promise from La Montagne to actually expose themselves, that is, to get out of the confines of the parliamentary struggle, in case their act of accusation was rejected. Throughout June 13, the proletariat retained this attitude of skeptical observation and awaited an inevitable, seriously compromising, and pointless body-to-body between the Democratic National Guard and the army, in order to then launch into battle and quickly take the revolution beyond the petty-bourgeois objective they had set for it. In the event of victory, the proletarian Commune had already been formed, which was to stand alongside the official government. The Parisian workers had learned the bloody lesson of June 1848.

On June 12, Minister Lacrosse personally made to the legislative Assembly the proposal that the act of indictment be passed immediately for discussion. During the night, the Government had made all the arrangements for defense and attack; the majority of the National Assembly was resolved to throw the rebellious minority out into the street, the minority itself could no longer retreat, the die was cast, three hundred and seventy-seven votes against eight rejected the indictment, La Montagne, who had abstained from voting, rushed grumbling into the propaganda hall and into the offices of "peaceful democracy". Once away from the parliamentary building, she lost her strength, just as the giant Anteus lost his strength whenever he moved away from his mother, the Earth. Sanctions within the confines of the legislative assembly, they were just philistines within the confines of "peaceful Democracy". A debate unfolded, long, noisy, empty. La Montagne was resolved to enforce respect for the Constitution by all means, "except by force of arms." She was supported in her decision by a manifesto and a delegation of "Friends of the Constitution." "Friends of the Constitution", so called the ruins of the "little church" at the National, of the bourgeois republican party. While, of its remaining parliamentary representatives, six had voted against the rejection of the act of indictment and all the others in favor, while Cavaignac put his saber to the disposal of the party of order, the greater extra-parliamentary part of the "little church" eagerly seized the occasion to get out of their position of political pariah and to enter en masse into the ranks of the Democratic Party. Did they not seem like natural heralds of that Party that hid behind its shield, under its principle, under the Constitution?

La Montagne stayed at work until dawn. She gave birth to a "proclamation to the people" which appeared on the morning of June 13 in two socialist newspapers, in a more or less humiliating place. It declared the president, the ministers, the majority of the legislative assembly "outside the constitution" and invited the national guard, the army and finally also the people "to revolt." "Long live the constitution!", was the slogan launched, a slogan that meant nothing but "Down with the revolution!"

This constitutional proclamation of La Montagne was followed on June 13 by what might be called a peaceful demonstration of the petty bourgeois, that is to say, a march from the Château-dEau through the boulevards: thirty thousand men, mostly of the National Guard, unarmed, mixed with members of secret workers' sections, parading to the cries of "Long live the Constitution! ", uttered in a mechanical, glacial manner by the marchers themselves, and which the echo of the people rushing onto the sidewalks repeated ironically instead of thickening, like thunder. This chant of multiple voices lacked the voice of the heart. And when the procession passed in front of the headquarters of the "Friends of the Constitution" and a herald in the pay of the Constitution appeared on top of the house, who, breaking the air with a decisive gesture of his tall hat, rained from his cyclopean lungs, like a hailstorm on the heads of the pilgrims, the slogan: "Long live the Constitution!", these same pilgrims seemed for an instant overcome by the comical situation. It is known that the procession reached the bouleoarês, at the entrance to the Rue de Ia Paix was received in a very unparliamentary manner by Changarnier's dragoons and hunters, and dispersed in all directions, still throwing behind them a few rickety cries of "The arms!" in order to complete the parliamentary call to arms of June 11.

The majority of La Montagne, gathered on the Rue du Hasard, disappeared when this brutal dispersal of the peaceful parade, confused rumors of the murder of unarmed citizens on the boulevards, the growing tumult in the street, all seemed to announce the proximity of a riot. At the head of a small group of deputies, Ledru-Rollin saved the honor of La Montagme. Under the protection of the artillery of Paris, which had united at the national Palace, they headed for the Conservatoire des Arts et Métiers, where the fifth and sixth legions were to arrive. But it was in vain that the Montagnards waited for the fifth and sixth legions: these prudent national guards left their representatives in doubt, the Paris artillery itself prevented the people from re-erecting barricades, a confused chaos made any decision impossible, the line troops advanced, bayonets crossed, one part of the representatives was taken prisoner, the other part escaped. Thus ends June 13.

If June 23, 1848 was the insurrection of the revolutionary proletariat, June 13, 1848 was the insurrection of the petty bourgeois democrats, each of these two insurrections being the pure, typical expression of the class that led it.

Only in Lyon did a bloody and bloody conflict break out. In that city where the bourgeoisie and the proletariat are directly face to face, where the workers' movement is not, as in Paris, involved and determined by the general movement, June 13 has consequently lost its primitive character. In the places in the province, however, where it exploded, it did not ignite - it was a flash of enthusiasm.

June 13 closed the first period of existence of the constitutional Republic which had begun its normal life on May 29, 1849, with the meeting of the legislative Assembly. The whole time that this prologue lasted is filled with the noisy struggle between the party of order and La Montagne, between the bourgeoisie and the petty bourgeoisie that is uselessly angry against the establishment of the bourgeois Republic in favor of which it had itself conspired, uninterruptedly, in the provisional government and in the executive committee, and for which it had fought fanatically against the proletariat during the June days. June 13 broke her resistance and made the legislative dictatorship of the Unified Monarchists a fait accompli. From that moment on, the National Assembly is merely the public security committee of the party of order.

Paris had put the president, the ministers and the majority of the National Assembly under "indictment"; these saw Paris in a "state of siege". La Montagne had declared the majority of the Assembly "outside the Constitution"; the majority cited La Montagne before the High Court for violation of the Constitution, and outlawed everything that was still vigorous within it. They weakened it to the point of reducing it to a trunk without head or heart. The minority had even attempted a parliamentary insurrection; the majority raised its parliamentary despotism to the level of a law. It enacted a new regulation that suppressed the freedom of the tribune and empowered the president of the National Assembly to punish representatives for disturbing order by censure, fine, suspension of parliamentary immunity, temporary expulsion, and imprisonment. Over the log of La Montagne, the majority suspended not the sword, but the lash. What remained of La Montagne's deputies should, as a matter of honor, withdraw en masse. The dissolution of the party of order had been accelerated by such an act. It could only decompose into its original elements, from the moment that the appearance of an opposition no longer held them together.

At the same time as they were deprived of their parliamentary strength, the petty bourgeois democrats were deprived of their armed force, the Parisian artillery was dispensed with, as were the eighth, ninth and twelfth legions of the national guard.

On the other hand, the legion of high finance, which on June 13 had stormed the printing works of Boulé and Roux, smashed the presses, devastated the offices of the republican newspapers, arbitrarily arrested editors, typesetters, printers, dispatchers, and ushers, this legion received encouraging approval from the rostrum. Throughout the length and breadth of France the dissolution of all national guards suspected of republicanism was repeated.

A new law against the press, a new law against associations, a new law on the state of siege, the prisons of Paris overcrowded, the political refugees persecuted, all the newspapers outside the positions of the National suspended. Lyon and the five bordering departments handed over to the brutal chicanery of military despotism, the surrogates present everywhere, the multitude of officials already often so selected, once more selected, such as the inevitable platitudes which the victorious reaction repeats endlessly and which, after the massacres and the deportations of June, only deserve to be mentioned because this time they were directed against Paris, and also against the departments, against the proletariat and above all the middle classes.

The repressive laws that referred to the government's decision to proclaim a state of siege, further strangled the press, and suppressed the right of association, absorbed all the legislative activity of the National Assembly during the months of June, July, and August.

However, this epoch is characterized not by the exploration of fact but of principle, not by the decisions of the national assembly but by the exposition of the reasons for those decisions, not by reality but by the word, not by the word but by the intonation and gesture which animate the word. The insolent, disrespectful expression of monarchist opinions, the insults of a contemptuous superiority against the Republic, the dissemination with frivolous affectation of the projects of restoration, in a word, the fanfare violation of republican norms, give to this period its particular hue and color. "Long live the Constitution!", was the battle cry of the losers of June 13. The victors were then disconnected from the hypocrisy of constitutional, that is, republican, language. The counter-revolution had subjugated Hungary, Italy, and Germany, and the Restoration was already believed to be at the gates of France. A veritable competition began to see who would open the dance among the leaders of the fractions of the order, boasting of their monarchism in the Moniteur, confessing and repenting for the sins they might have committed for liberalism under the Republic and imploring God and man for forgiveness. Not a day went by without the tribune of the National Assembly declaring the revolution a public disgrace, without some legitimist nobleman from a province solemnly declaring that he had never recognized the Republic, without one of the deserters and poltroon traitors of the July monarchy extemporaneously recounting the heroic feats that only the philanthropy of Louis Philippe or other misunderstandings had prevented him from accomplishing. What should be admired in the February days was not the generosity of the victorious people, but the abnegation and moderation of the monarchists who had allowed them to win. A representative of the people proposed that part of the resources destined for the wounded of February should be allocated to the National Guards who, during those days, had so well honored the homeland. Another wanted a decree to erect an equestrian statue to the Duke of Orléans in the Place du Carrousel. Thiers called the Constitution a "dirty piece of paper. One after another there appeared on the rostrum Orléanists who regretted having conspired against the legitimate monarchy, legitimists who reproached themselves for having hastened the fall of the monarchy in general with their rebellion against the illegitimate monarchy. Thiers who lamented that he had intrigued against Molé, Molé against Guizot, Barrot against all three. The cry of "Long live the Social Democratic Republic!" was deemed unconstitutional. The cry of "Long live the Republic!" was accused of being social democratic. On the anniversary day of the battle of Waterloo, one representative declared, "I fear less the invasion of the Prussians than the return to France of the revolutionary exiles." The complaints against organized terrorism in Lyon and the neighboring departments, Baraguay dHilliers replied, "I prefer white terror to red terror." And the Assembly burst into frenzied applause each time an epigram against the Revolution, against the Republic, against the Constitution, in favor of the monarchy, in favor of the Holy Alliance, fell from the lips of its speakers. Every violation of the smallest republican formalities - not calling, for example, the representatives "citizens" - excited the gentlemen of the order.

The supplementary elections of July 8 in Paris, held under the influence of the state of siege and with the abstention of a large part of the proletariat, the occupation of Rome by the French army, the entrance in procession of the Red Eminences and, after them, of the Inquisition and the terrorism of the monks in Rome, all these events brought new victories to the June victory and increased the drunkenness of the party of order.

Finally, in the middle of August, half with the intention of attending the General Councils that were about to meet, half out of weariness at the ideological orgies that had lasted for many months, the monarchists decreed a two-month recess of the National Assembly. With visible irony, they left a commission of twenty-five representatives, the cream of the legitimists and Orleanists, a Molé, a Changarnier, as representatives of the National Assembly and guardians of the Republic. The irony was greater than they thought. Condemned by history to aid the overthrow of the monarchy they loved, they were appointed by it to preserve the Republic they hated.

With the recess of the legislative assembly, the second period of the constitutional republic's existence, its period of monarchist revelry, ended.

The state of siege in Paris once suspended, the action of the press was resumed. During the suspension of the social democratic newspapers, during the period of repressive legislation and monarchist insanities, the Siècle, the old literary representative of the constitutional monarchist petit bourgeois, became republicanized; La Presse, the old literary representative of the bourgeois reformers, became democratized; Le National, the old classic organ of the bourgeois republicans, became socialized.

Secret societies grew in extent and intensity as public political associations became impossible. Workers' industrial associations, tolerated as purely commercial societies, without any economic value, became, from a political point of view, also means of uniting the proletariat. The 13th of June had removed from the different semi-revolutionary parties their official leaders; the masses that remained gained thereby the advantage of acting on their own initiative. The gentlemen of order had intimidated by prophesying the horrors of the Red Republic; the gross excesses, the hyperbole atrocities of the victorious counter-revolution in Hungary, in Baden, in Rome, excused the "Red Republic." As for the discontented middle layers of French society, they were beginning to prefer the sermons of the Red Republic with its problematic atrocities to the atrocities of the white monarchy, with its character of royal despair. No socialist in France made more revolutionary propaganda than Haynau. To each capacity according to his works!

However, Louis Bonaparte took advantage of the vacations of the National Assembly to make princely trips to the provinces; the most ardent legitimists went on pilgrimage to Ems with the descendant of Saint Louis, and the multitude of representatives of the people, friends of order, made intrigues in the general councils that had just met. It was a matter of making them express what the majority of the national assembly did not yet dare to say, the declaration of the urgency of an immediate revision of the Constitution. Constitutionally, the Constitution could only be revised in 1852 and by a national Assembly specially convened for this purpose. But if the majority of the departmental councils had pronounced themselves in this sense, shouldn't the National Assembly, in the name of France, sacrifice the virginity of the Constitution? The national Assembly nurtured, with regard to these provincial assemblies, the same hopes as the nuns had with regard to the Pandours in Voltaire's Henriade. But the Putiphars of the national Assembly only had to deal, with a few exceptions, with so many other provincial Josephs. An overwhelming majority did not want to understand the hasty insinuation. The revision of the constitution was disgraced by the very instruments that were to bring it to life by the votes of the general councils. The voice of France, and indeed the voice of bourgeois France, had spoken and spoken out against the revision.

In early October, the national legislative assembly met again - tantum mutatus ab illo. Its physiognomy was radically changed. The rejection of revision by the general councils had brought it back within the limits of the Constitution and shown it the limits of its duration. The Orleanists had grown suspicious of the legitimists' pilgrimages to Ems, the legitimists suspicious of Orleanist talks with London, the newspapers of the two fractions were fanning the flames and weighing the reciprocal claims of their suitors; The Orleanists and Legitimists, united, held a grudge against the Bonapartists for their intrigues which revealed the princely journeys, the more or less visible attempts to emancipate the President, the pretentious language of the Bonapartist newspapers; Louis Bonaparte held a grudge against the National Assembly which only thought the Orleanist Legitimist conspiracy legitimate, and against a Ministry which constantly betrayed him in favor of the National Assembly. Finally, the ministry itself was divided on the Roman policy and on the income tax proposed by Minister Passy and denounced as socialist by the conservatives.

One of the first proposals of the Barrot ministry to the reconvened legislative assembly was a request for a credit of three hundred thousand francs to constitute a dowry for the duchess of Orléans. The National Assembly agreed, thus adding to the French nation's record of debts a sum of seven million francs. Thus, while Louis-Philippe continued to successfully play the role of the "superb poor man," the ministry did not dare to propose a salary increase in Bonaparte's favor, and the Assembly did not seem willing to agree to it. And Louis Bonaparte hesitated, as always, before the dilemma: Aut Caesar, aut Clichy.

The second ministerial request for credit of nine million francs to pay the expenses of the Rome expedition increased the tension between Bonaparte and the ministers of the National Assembly. Louis Bonaparte had caused a letter to appear in Le Moniteur to his officer-ordainant, Edgar Ney, in which he bound the pontifical government to constitutional guarantees. The pope, for his part, had issued a bull - motu proprio - in which he rejected any restrictions on his restored power. With his letter, Bonaparte was, by a deliberate indiscretion, lifting the curtain of his office, to pose himself before the gallery as a genius full of good will but wronged, and a prisoner within his own house. It was not the first time he had acted, full of affectation, with the "furtive flapping of wings of a free soul." Thiers, the commission's rapporteur, completely ignored Napoleon's wing flapping and contented himself with translating the pontifical text into French. It was not the ministry, but Victor Hugo, who tried to save the president with an agenda that the Assembly should approve Napoleon's letter. Let's go! Let's go! It was with this cold and disrespectful interjection that the majority buried Victor Hugo's proposal. The president's policy? The president's letter? The president himself? Let's go! Let's go! Who the hell takes Monsieur Bonaparte seriously? Do you believe, Monsieur Victor Hugo, that we believe when you say you believe the president? Let's go! Let's go!

Finally, the rupture between Bonaparte and the National Assembly was precipitated by the discussion about the return of the Orléans and the Bourbons. In the absence of the ministry, the President's cousin, son of the former King of Westphalia, had put forward this proposal whose sole purpose was to bring the legitimist and Orleanist suitors down to the same level, or lower, preferably, than that of the Bonapartist suitor, since the latter, at least, was in fact at the summit of power.

Napoleon Bonaparte was irreverent enough to make the return of the exiled royal families, and the amnesty of the June insurgents, the articles of a single proposition. The indignation of the majority immediately forced him to ask pardon for this criminal linking of the sacred to the infamous, of the royal strains to the proletarian rabble, of the fixed stars of society to the fatuous fires of their swamps, and to give each of the two propositions the value it deserved. The National Assembly vigorously rejected the return of the royal family, and Berryer, the Demosthenes of the legitimists, left no doubt as to the significance of that vote. The bourgeois degradation of the suitors, that is the desired goal. The desire is to rob them of their halo, their last remaining majesty, the majesty of exile! What would you think, cried Berryer, of these suitors who, having forgotten their illustrious origin, would return to live here as simple citizens! Louis Bonaparte could not be told more clearly that his presence had gained him nothing, and that if the coalition monarchists needed him in France as a neutral man sitting in the presidential chair, the serious pretenders to the crown should remain hidden from unholy eyes by the clouds of exile.

On November 1, Louis Bonaparte responded to the Legislative Assembly with a message announcing, in rather blunt terms, the dismissal of the Barrot ministry and the constitution of a new ministry. The Barrot-Falloux ministry was the ministry of the monarchist coalition, the Hautpoul ministry was the ministry of Bonaparte, the organ of the president, before the legislative assembly, the ministry of the subordinate employees.

Bonaparte was no longer the simply neutral man of December 10, 1848. The possession of executive power had grouped around him numerous interests, the struggle against anarchy obliged the party of order itself to increase its influence, and if Bonaparte was no longer popular, the party of order was unpopular. Faced with the Orleanists and the Legitimists, could he not hope, thanks to their rivalry and the necessity of some sort of monarchist restoration, to oblige them to recognize the neutral pretender?

It is November 1, 1849 that dates the third period of existence of the constitutional republic, a period that ends on March 10, 1850. It is not only through the regular play of constitutional institutions, so admired by Guizot, that the dispute between executive and legislative power begins. Before the yearnings for restoration of the coalition of Orleanists and legitimists, Bonaparte represents the title of his royal power, the Republic; before Bonaparte's yearnings for restoration, the party of order represents the title of its common domination, the Republic; before the Orleanists, the legitimists, the Orleanists represent the status quo, the Republic. All these fractions of the party of order, where each has, in petto, its own king and its own restoration, make the common domination of the bourgeoisie, the form under which particular pretensions are neutralized and set aside - the Republic - prevail alternatively, in the face of their rivals' yearnings for usurpation and removal. Just as Kant made the Republic, the only rational form of State, a postulate of practical reason, the realization of which is never attained, but which must be constantly sought as a goal and always kept in mind, so these monarchists make the monarchy a postulate.

Thus, the constitutional republic, which came out of the hands of the bourgeois republicans as an empty ideological formula, became in the hands of the coalition monarchists a living form rich in content. And Thiers was telling a greater truth than he thought when he declared, "It is we monarchists who are the real supports of the constitutional Republic."

The fall of the coalition ministry, the taking over of the ministry of subordinate employees has a second significance. His minister of finance was called Fould. Fould, minister of finance, is the official handing over of the French national wealth to the Stock Exchange, it is the administration of political fortunes by the Stock Exchange and in the interests of the Stock Exchange. With Fould's appointment, the financial aristocracy announced its restoration in Le Moniteur. This restoration necessarily completed the others that constitute, as it were, links in the chain of the constitutional Republic.

Louis-Philippe had never dared to make a true lynx a minister of finance. Even if his monarchy was the ideal name for the domination of the upper bourgeoisie, the privileged interests in his ministries had to bear the names of a disinterested ideology. The bourgeois Republic everywhere thrust into the foreground what the various monarchies, both legitimist and Orleanist, were carrying hidden behind the scenes. It brought down to earth what they had divinized. It put the bourgeois proper names of the ruling class interests in the place of the names of their saints.

Our entire exposition has shown that the Republic, from the first day of its existence, did not overthrow but, on the contrary, constituted the financial aristocracy. But the concessions made to it were a destiny to which it submitted without wanting to bring it into being. With Fould, government initiative became financial aristocracy.

One wonders how the coalition bourgeoisie could support and tolerate the domination of finance which, under Louis Philippe, rested on the exclusion or subordination of the other bourgeois fractions?

The answer is simple.

First of all, the financial aristocracy itself constitutes a group of preponderant importance in the monarchist coalition, whose common governmental power is called the Republic. Are not the coryphons and luminaries of the Orleanists the former allies and accomplices of the financial aristocracy? Is it not the golden phalanx of Orleanism? As for the legitimists, under Louis Philippe they had already been involved in all the orgies of stock market, mining, and railroad speculation. In short, the union of large property holdings with high finance is a normal fact. England and Austria themselves prove it.

In a country like France, where the importance of national production is immensely inferior to that of the national debt, where the income of the State constitutes the most important object of speculation, and where the Stock Exchange forms the principal market for the investment of capital that wants to invest productively, in such a country it is necessary that an enormous multitude of people of all the bourgeois or semi-bourgeois classes participate in public debt, in the game of the Stock Exchange, in finance. Don't all these subordinate participants find their support and their natural leaders in the fraction that represents these interests in the most massive proportions, and that represents them in their totality?

What determines the fact that the public fortune falls into the hands of high finance? The ever-increasing indebtedness of the state. And the indebtedness of the state? The continuous exceeding of expenditure over revenue, a disproportion that is both cause and effect of the system of public loans.

In order to escape this indebtedness, it is necessary that the state restrict its expenditures, that is, simplify, reduce the governmental machine, govern as little as possible, relate as little as possible to bourgeois society. An impossible thing for the party of order, whose means of repression, whose official intrusion in the name of the State, whose presence everywhere through State bodies had necessarily to increase as its domination and the conditions of existence of its class were threatened on all sides. One cannot reduce one's guard when attacks against people and property multiply.

Or else it is necessary for the state to try to avoid debts and reach an instantaneous, albeit temporary, equilibrium in the budget by placing extraordinary contributions on the shoulders of the wealthier classes. In order to subtract the national wealth from the exploitation of the stock market, the party of order should sacrifice its own fortune on the altar of the fatherland? Let's not be naïve!

So, no complete transformation of the French state, no transformation of the French budget. With the current budget, need for the indebtedness of the state, and, with the indebtedness of the state, need for the domination of commerce, public debts, the creditors of the state, the bankers, the money dealers, the lynchpins. Only a fraction of the party of order took part directly in the overthrow of the financial aristocracy: the manufacturers. We are not talking about the average industrialists, nor the small ones, but the administrators of the factory interests that had, under Louis Philip, formed the great base of the dynastic opposition. Their interest is unquestionably the reduction of production expenses, therefore the reduction of taxes that go into production, therefore the reduction of public debts whose interest goes into taxes, therefore the overthrow of the financial aristocracy.

In England - and the biggest French manufacturers are nothing but petty bourgeois alongside their English rivals - we really find manufacturers, a Cobden, a Bright, at the head of the crusade against the bank and the stock market aristocracy. Why doesn't this happen in France? In England, it is industry that predominates; in France, it is agriculture. In England, industry needs free trade; in France, it needs duaneira protection, the national monopoly alongside other monopolies. French industry does not dominate French production, French industrialists, as a consequence, do not dominate the French bourgeoisie. To make their interests triumph against the other fractions of the bourgeoisie, they cannot, like the English, put themselves at the head of the movement and carry at the same time their class interests to the extreme; they must follow the revolution and serve interests which are contrary to the general interests of their class. In February they had neglected their position; February has made them prudent people. And who is more directly threatened by the workers than the employer, the industrial capitalist? This is why the manufacturer has necessarily become, in France, the most fanatical member of the party of order. The diminution of his profit by finance, what is it compared with the annulment of profit by the proletariat?

In France, the petty bourgeois does what the industrial bourgeois should normally do; the worker does what would normally be the task of the petty bourgeois; and the worker's task, who performs it? Nobody. In France, the task is not performed; in France, it is proclaimed. It is not accomplished anywhere within the confines of the nation; the class war within French society has expanded into a world war where nations meet face to face. The solution only approaches the moment when, by the world war, the proletarian finds himself at the head of the people who dominate the world market, at the head of England. The revolution finding there not its end, but a beginning of organization, is not a short-lived revolution. The present generation resembles the Jews that Moses led through the desert. It has not only a new world to conquer; it must disappear to make room for men who will be equal to the new world.

Let's go back to Fould.

On November 14, 1849, Fould took to the rostrum of the National Assembly and laid out his financial system: apologia for the old tax system, maintenance of the liquor tax, withdrawal of the Passy income tax!

And yet Passy was not a revolutionary, he was a former minister of Louis-Philippe. He was one of those puritanical types of Dufaure's force, one of those most intimate confidants of Test, the July monarchy scapegoat. Passy, he too, had paid lip service to the old tax system, recommended maintaining the liquor tax, but had at the same time torn the veil from the public deficit. He had explained the need for a new income tax if one did not want to go into public bankruptcy. Fould, who had advised Ledru-Rollin on bankruptcy, interceded with the Legislature on behalf of the state deficit. He promised savings, the secret of which was later revealed: we saw, for example, expenses decrease by sixty million and the floating debt grow by two hundred million - a magic trick in the articulation of numbers, in the establishment of the accounts that all lead, finally, to new loans.

With Fould, the financial aristocracy, alongside the other bourgeois fractions that envied it, did not show, of course, as much cynical corruption as in the time of Louis-Philippe. But the system remained the same: constant increase of debts, concealment of the deficit. Then, over time, the stock market scrounging of old manifested itself with greater cynicism. The law on the Avignon railroad, the mysterious fluctuations of state values, of which all Paris spoke for some time, finally, the unfortunate speculations of Fould and Bonaparte about the March 10 elections, prove this.

With the official restoration of the financial aristocracy, the French people could not but find themselves on the eve of a new February 24th.

In a fit of misanthropy against its heiress, the Constituent Assembly had abolished the liquor tax for the year of grace 1850. It was not by suppressing old taxes that new debts could be paid. Créton, a cretin of the party of order, had proposed maintaining the liquor tax even before the legislative assembly prorogued. Fould took up this proposal on behalf of the Bonapartist ministry, and on December 20, 1849, the anniversary of Bonaparte's proclamation, the national Assembly decided on the reinstatement of the liquor tax.

The first speaker in favor of this decision was not a financier, but the leader of the Jesuits, Montalembert. His deduction was of an impressive simplicity: the tax is the teat where the government sucks. The government is the instruments of repression, the organs of authority, the army, the police, the officials, the judges, the ministers, the priests. The attack against the tax is the anarchists' attack against the sentinels of order, who protect the material and spiritual production of bourgeois society against the incursions of the proletarian vandals. The tax is the fifth deity, next to property, family, order and religion. So the liquor tax is unquestionably a tax, and moreover, it is not an ordinary tax, but a traditional, monarchist-minded, respectable tax. Long live the beverage tax! Three cheers and one cheer more!

The peasant, when he evokes the devil, gives him the traits of the bailiff, bringer of disquiet. From the moment Montalembert made the tax a god, the peasant became ungodly, an atheist, and threw himself into the arms of the devil, socialism. The order religion had mocked him, the Jesuits had mocked him, Bonaparte had mocked him. December 20, 1849 had irretrievably compromised December 20, 1848. The "nephew of his uncle" was no longer the first of his family who had been defeated by the liquor tax, by that tax which, according to Montalembert's expression, "announces the revolutionary storm." The real, great Napoleon declared in Saint Helena that the re-establishment of the liquor tax had contributed more to his downfall than anything else, leading him to win the hostility of the peasants of midi France. Already the object of popular anger under Louis XIV (see the works of Boisguillebert and de Vauban), abolished by the first revolution, it was re-established in 1808 by Napoleon in a new form. When the Restoration came to France, not only were the Cossacks galloping before it, but also the solemn proceedings to abolish the liquor tax. Of course, the nobility did not have to keep their word before the "gent taillable à merci et miséricorde"; 1830 promised the suppression of the liquor tax. It was not in their nature to do what they said and say what they did; 1848 promised the abolition of the liquor tax as they promised everything. Finally, the Constitution, which promised nothing, had, as we said before, a testamentary attitude that the liquor tax should disappear on January 1, 1850. And it was precisely ten days before January 1, 1850 that the Legislative reinstated it. So the French people continually gave him chase, and when he went out the door, they saw him come in through the window.

The popular hatred of the beverage tax is explained by the fact that it brings together all the odious sides of the French tax system. Its mode of collection is odious, its mode of distribution is aristocratic, since the percentages of the tax are the same for the most ordinary and for the finest wines, it then increases in geometric proportion as the fortune of the consumers decreases, it is a progressive tax in reverse. It also directly causes the poisoning of the working classes, making counterfeit and manufactured wines more sought after. He diminishes consumption by erecting tax points at the entrance of all towns with more than four thousand inhabitants and turning them into a kind of foreign country by anticipating the duane rights on French wine. So the big wine merchants, even more the small ones, the wine sellers, are also declared opponents of the liquor tax. And finally, by decreasing consumption, the beverage tax robs production of its market. At the same time that it puts city workers in the position of being unable to pay for wine, it puts wine growers in the position of being unable to sell it. Now, France has a population of twelve million winegrowers. One can immediately understand the hatred of the people in general; one can especially understand the fanaticism of the peasants against the liquor tax. Moreover, in their re-establishment, the peasants did not see an isolated, more or less accidental fact. They have a sort of historical tradition that is handed down from father to son: in this school of history, it is whispered by the ear that every government, when it wants to deceive the peasants, promises the suppression of the liquor tax; and that, as soon as it gets what it wants, it keeps it or reinstates it. It is in the liquor tax that the peasant recognizes the "aroma" of the government, its orientation. The reinstatement of this tax on December 20 meant: Louis Bonaparte is like the others; but he was not like the others, he was an invention of the peasants, and in the petitions against the liquor tax, which had millions of signatures, they collected the votes they had given, a year before, to "their uncle's nephew.

The peasant population, which exceeds two-thirds of the French population, is mostly made up of supposedly free landowners. The first generation, freed by the Revolution of 1789 from feudal burdens, had paid nothing for the land. But the following generations paid, in the form of land value, what their semi- serf ancestors had paid in the form of rent, tithes, corvees, etc. The more the population grew, the more the share of land increased and the more the price of the lot rose, as demand grew as its size decreased. The more the price the peasant paid for a plot increased, either by having bought it directly or by having it counted as capital by his co-defendants, the more the peasant's indebtedness, that is, the mortgage, increased in the same proportion. The title of credit made over the land is called, in effect, mortgage, a guarantee over the land. Just as privileges accumulated on medieval property, mortgages accumulated on the modern lot. On the other hand, in the allotment regime, land is for its owner a mere instrument of production. As the land is fragmented, its fertility decreases. The use of machinery on the land, the division of labor, the great works of soil improvement, such as canals, drainage, irrigation, etc., become more and more impossible, while the incidental expenses of cultivation grow in proportion to the division of the instrument of production itself. And this is how much capital the plot owner does or does not possess. The more the division increases, and the more the property constitutes with its extremely miserable inventory all the capital of the peasant plotter; and the less the capital is invested in the land, and the more the small peasant lacks land, money, and the knowledge to utilize the advances of agronomy; and the more the culture of the soil regresses. Finally, the net product decreases as gross consumption grows, and the peasant's entire family is taken away from any other occupation by his property, and he is not even able to support it.

It is then as the population grows, and with it the sharing of land, that the instrument of production, the land, becomes more expensive, and its fertility decreases; it is in the same measure that agriculture declines and the peasant becomes indebted. And what was the effect becomes, in turn, the cause; Each generation leaves the other more in debt, each new generation begins under the most unfavorable and harshest conditions, mortgage begets mortgage, and when the peasant can no longer offer his land in pledge of new debts, that is, the burden of new mortgages, he becomes directly prey to usury; and the usurious interest becomes greater and greater.

It then happens that the French peasant, in the form of interest on the mortgages made on the land, in the form of interest on the usurers' unmortgaged advances, yields to the capitalist not only the land rent, not only the industrial profit, in a word, not only all the net benefits, but even a part of the wage, so that he falls to the level of the Irish farmer; and all this under the pretext of being a private owner.

This process has been accelerated in France by the ever-increasing tax burdens and the expense of justice, whether it comes directly from the very formalities with which French law surrounds immovable property, or from the innumerable conflicts caused by lots that everywhere touch and confuse each other, or from the progressive fury of the peasants whose enjoyment of society is limited to fanatically enforcing their imaginary property, the right of ownership.

According to a statistical table dating from 1840, the gross product of the soil in France amounts to five billion, two hundred thirty-seven million, one hundred seventy-eight thousand francs. From this, three billion, five hundred and fifty-two million francs must be deducted for the expenses of cultivating the land, including the feeding of the men who work it. This leaves a net product of one billion six hundred and eighty-five million one hundred and seventy-eight thousand francs, from which must be deducted five hundred and fifty million francs for mortgage interest, one hundred million francs for justice officials, three hundred and fifty million francs for registration fees, franchise fees, mortgages, etc. That leaves one-third of the net product, five hundred and thirty-eight million; divided per capita of the population, it is not even twenty-five francs net product. Naturally, this calculation does not include non-mortgage usury, lawyer's fees, etc.

It will be understood what was the situation of the French peasants when the Republic added new burdens to the existing ones. It will be seen that their exploitation differs only in form from the exploitation of the industrial proletariat. The exploiter is the same: Capital. The capitalists, properly speaking, exploit the peasants, properly speaking, through mortgages and usury. The capitalist class exploits the peasant class through the state tax. The property title is the talisman with which capital has hitherto bewitched it, the pretext under which it has incited it against the industrial proletariat. Only the fall of capital can raise the peasant, only an anti-capitalist, proletarian government can lift him out of his economic misery, out of his social degradation. The constitutional republic is the dictatorship of its coalition exploiters, the social democratic republic, the red republic, is the dictatorship of its allies. And the scales rise or fall according to the votes that the peasant throws into the ballot box. It is up to him to decide his own fate. This is what the socialists said in pamphlets, almanacs, calendars, leaflets of all kinds. This language was made more comprehensible to the peasant thanks to the opposing publications of the party of order, which addressed him in turn, with crude exaggeration, brutal interpretation and representation of the intentions and ideas of the socialists, struck the right tone in the peasant and aroused the desire for the forbidden fruit. But the most understandable language was the peasant class's own experiences of exercising the right to vote, and the disappointments that, in the revolutionary fallout, had continually befallen it. Revolutions are the locomotive of history.

The gradual agitation manifested itself among the peasants through different symptoms. It showed itself already in the elections to the Legislative Assembly, it showed itself in the state of siege proclaimed in the five departments bordering Lyon; it showed itself a few months after June 13 with the election of a Montagnard in place of the former mayor, who is nowhere to be found in the department of Gironde; It showed itself on December 20, 1849, with the election of a red deputy in place of a deceased legitimist in the Gard department, this promised land of the legitimists, theater of the most terrible crimes against the republicans in 1794 and 1795, center of the white terror in 1815, when liberals and protestants were publicly murdered. It was after the re-establishment of the liquor tax that this revolution of the most accommodating class manifested itself in the most visible way. The government measures and laws of January and February 1850 were almost exclusively directed against the departments and the peasants. This is the most impressive proof of their progress.

Hautpoul's circular making the gendarme the inquisitor of the prefect, the sub-prefect and above all the maire, who organized spies even in the farthest corners of the rural commune; the law against the teachers, which subjected them, the luminaries, spokesmen, educators and interpreters of the peasant class, to the arbitrary rule of the prefect who hunted them down from one to another like an animal to be hunted, these proletarians of the educated class; the proposed law against the minors, which raised above their heads the sword of the Democles of the revolution, and which at every moment confronted them, the presidents of the communes, with the president of the Republic and the party of order; the order which transformed the seventeen military regions of France into four paxaliques and which granted the French the barracks and the camp as their national salon; the law on education, by which the party of order proclaimed that the unconsciousness and the coarsening of France by force are the condition of her existence. What were all these laws and measures? Forms of desperate attempts by the party of order to win back the departments and the peasants of the departments.

Considered as means of repression, they were pitiful and ran counter to their own purpose. The great measures like the maintenance of the liquor tax, the forty-five cent tax, the scornful rejection of the peasants' petitions for the refund of the billions, etc., all these legislative rays from the center fell on the abandoned peasant class like a whip; the laws and measures mentioned made attack and resistance the general daily conversation in every hovel, inoculating the revolution into every village; they localized the revolution and made it peasant.

On the other hand, do not these proposals of Bonaparte, their adoption by the national Assembly, prove the union of the two powers of the constitutional Republic, at least when it is a question of the repression of anarchy, or rather of all the classes which rise up against the bourgeois dictatorship? Had not Soulouque, immediately after his abrupt message, assured the Legislative of his devotion to order by means of Carlíer's message, this obscene, crude caricature of Fouché, as Louis Bonaparte himself was the vulgar caricature of Napoleon?

The teaching law shows us the alliance of the young Catholics and the old Voltaireans. Could the domination of the united bourgeois be anything other than the coalition despotism of the Jesuit-friendly Restoration and the July monarchy thinking itself above good and evil? The weapons that one of the bourgeois fractions had distributed among the people against the other in their reciprocal struggles for supremacy, did it not have to be taken back from the people when the latter began to oppose their combined dictatorship? Nothing irritated Parisian commerce more than this affected display of Jesuitism, not even the rejection of friendly concordats. Meanwhile, coalitions continued as well among the different fractions of the party of order as between the national Assembly and Bonaparte. It did not please the National Assembly very much that Bonaparte, immediately after his coup d'état, after the formation of his own Bonapartist ministry, had summoned before him the powerless of the monarchy, now appointed prefects, and made their anti-constitutional agitation in favor of his re-election to the presidency the condition for keeping them in their functions; that Carlier had celebrated his inauguration with the extinction of a legitimist political association; that Napoleon had founded his own newspaper, the Napoléon, which revealed to the public the president's secret ambitions, while his ministers were obliged to deny them on the rostrum of the Legislative; She was not pleased either with this insolent maintenance of the ministry despite numerous votes of no confidence, nor with the attempt to gain the support of non-commissioned officers through a high daily salary of four sous, and the support of the proletariat through a kind of plagiarism of Eugene Sue's Mysteres, the bank of interest-free loans; displeasure, finally, at the insolence with which the ministers were proposing the deportation to Algeria of the last of the June insurrectionists, in order to cast wholesale unpopularity on the legislative representatives, while the President was reserving retail popularity for himself with a few acts of benevolence. Thiers unleashed threatening words of coups d'etat and frivolous decisions, and the Legislature took its revenge by rejecting any bill he personally introduced, and by submitting to a noisy inquiry, full of suspicion, every one of those he made in the general interest, to see if, by increasing executive power, he did not aim at the profit of personal power. In short, she would take revenge with the conspiracy of indifference. The Legitimist party, for its part, watched with displeasure as the more capable Orleanists again seized almost all the posts and centralization grew, while it sought its security in decentralization on principle. And it was true. The counter-revolution centralized by force, that is, it prepared the mechanism of the revolution. Through the forced course of bank notes, it centralized even the gold and silver of France in the Bank of Paris, thus creating the prepared war treasury of the revolution.

The Orleanists, finally, noted with disgust that the principle of legitimacy was being opposed to their principle of gentrification, and they found themselves neglected and mistreated at every turn like a noble husband married to a bourgeois woman.

We have seen the peasants, the petty bourgeoisie, the middle classes in general, progressively pass over to the sides of the proletariat, brought into open opposition against the official Republic, treated by it as adversaries. Revolt against the bourgeois dictatorship, the need to change society, the maintenance of the republican-democratic institutions as its motor organs, the grouping around the proletariat as the decisive revolutionary force - such are the common features of what is called the party of social democracy, the party of the red republic. This party of anarchy, as its opponents have christened it, is as much a coalition of different interests as the party of order. From the minor reform of the old social disorder to the subversion of this old social order, from bourgeois liberalism to revolutionary terrorism, these are the extreme points that constitute at the same time the starting point and the terminal point of the party of "anarchy.

The suppression of protectionist rights - that's socialism! because it opposes the monopoly of the industrial fraction of the party of order. The regularization of the state budget - is socialism! because it opposes the monopoly of the financial fraction of the party of order. The free access of foreign meat and grain - it is socialism!, because it opposes the monopoly of the third fraction of the party of order, the large landowners. The demands of the free-chambist party, that is, of the most advanced English bourgeois party, appeared in France also as socialist demands. Voltaireanism - it is socialism! because it opposes a fourth fraction of the party of order, the Catholic fraction. Freedom of the press, right of association, general instruction of the people, that's socialism, still socialism! They oppose the monopoly of the party of order as a whole.

The march of the revolution had so quickly brought the situation to maturity that the friends of reform of all kinds, that the most modest demands of the middle classes, were forced to rally around the banner of the most radical subversive party, the Red Flag.

However varied, moreover, the socialism of the various large fractions of the party of anarchy, according to the economic conditions and all the revolutionary needs of their class or class fraction, were in agreement on one point: they proclaimed that it was the means of emancipation of the owner and that the emancipation of the owner was its goal. Deliberate lie for some, illusion for others, who proclaim the world transformed to their needs as the best of worlds for all, as the fulfillment of all revolutionary demands, and the suppression of all revolutionary coalitions.

Under the socialist words in general quite similar to those of the party of anarchy, hides the socialism of the National, of La Presse and of the Siêcle, which wants, in a more or less consequential manner, to overthrow the domination of the financial aristocracy and to free industry and commerce from their old chains. It is the socialism of industry, commerce and agriculture, whose administrators of the party of order renege on interests as they no longer accord with their private monopolies. From this bourgeois socialism, which naturally, like every variety of socialism, brings together a portion of workers and petty bourgeoisie, is distinguished petty bourgeois socialism proper, the socialism par excellence. Capital pursues this class mainly as a creditor: it demands credit institutions; it crushes it through competition, it demands associations subsidized by the State; it oppresses it through concentration, it demands progressive taxes, restrictions on inheritance, the execution by the State of large works and other measures that violently hinder the growth of capital. Since she dreams of a peaceful realization of her socialism - except, perhaps, a second February revolution of a few days - the next historical process naturally seems to her the application of systems that social thinkers conceive or have conceived together or in isolation. The petty bourgeois thus become heathens or adherents of existing socialist systems, of the doctrinal socialism that has been the theoretical expression of the proletariat for so long that it, the proletariat, was not yet developed enough to become a free and independent historical movement.

Thus, while utopia, doctrinaire socialism which subordinates the whole movement to one of its moments, which puts in the place of common, social production the cerebral activity of the individual pedant and whose fantasy suppresses the revolutionary struggle of the classes with their needs, by means of small artifices or great sentimentalisms, while this doctrinaire socialism which limits itself at bottom to idealizing current society, to reproducing to it an image without any shadow and which wishes to make its ideal triumph over social reality; while the proletariat leaves this socialism to the petty bourgeoisie, while the struggle of the different systems among themselves makes each of the alleged systems appear as the pretentious maintenance of one of the transition points of social agitation against another point, the proletariat unites more and more around revolutionary socialism, around the communism to which the bourgeoisie itself has given the name of Blanqui. This socialism is the permanent declaration of the revolution, the class dictatorship of the proletariat, the necessary transition to arrive at the extinction of the different classes in general, the extinction of all the relations of production on which they rest, the extinction of all the social relations that correspond to those relations of production, the subversion of all the ideas that emanate from those social relations.

The space reserved for this exposition does not allow us to develop this subject sufficiently.

We have seen that, if within the party of order it was the financial aristocracy that necessarily took the lead, in the party of "anarchy" it was the proletariat. While the various classes united in a revolutionary league were grouped around the proletariat, while the departments became less and less secure and the legislative assembly itself became more and more irritated by the pretensions of the French Soulouque, the complementary elections, so long postponed and delayed to replace the proscribed montagnards of June 13, were approaching.

Scorned by its enemies, mistreated and daily humiliated by its so-called friends, the Government saw only one way out of its repugnant and unbearable situation: rioting. A riot in Paris would allow it to proclaim a state of siege in the capital and the departments and thus give it command of the elections. On the other hand, the friends of order, faced with a government that had achieved victory over anarchy, would be forced to make concessions, if they did not want to appear as anarchists themselves.

The government set to work. In early February 1850, it provoked the people by felling the trees of liberty. Once the trees of liberty were gone, the Government itself lost its head and retreated, frightened at his provocation. But the national Assembly received this clumsy attempt at Bonaparte's emancipation with a glacial distrust. The removal of the crowns of the immortals on the July obelisk was no more successful. It provided a part of the army with the occasion for revolutionary demonstrations, and the national Assembly with the pretext for a more or less disguised vote of no confidence against the ministry. And it was in vain that the government press threatened with the suppression of universal suffrage, the invasion of the Cossacks. Houtpoul uselessly invited, in the middle of the Legislative, the left to come down to the street, declaring that the Government was willing to receive it. Haultpoul obtained nothing but a call to order from the President, and the party of order let, with a secret malignant glee, a deputy of the left ridicule Bonaparte's usurping ambitions. Unhelpfully, at last, a revolution was prophesied for February 24. The Government arranged for February 24th to be ignored by the people.

The proletariat would not allow itself to be provoked into any agitation, because it was on the verge of making a revolution.

Undeterred by the government's provocations, which only increased the general anger at the prevailing state of affairs, the electoral committee, which was under the influence of the workers, put forward three candidates for Paris: Deflotte, Vidal and Carnot. Deflotte was a June deportee, amnestied by Napoleon in an act aimed at popularity, was a friend of Blanqui and had taken part in the May 15 attack; Vidal, Louis Blanc's former secretary on the Luxembourg commission, was known as a communist writer for his book De la répartition des richesses; Carnot, son of the conventional who had organized the victory, the least compromised of the party members of the National, had been Minister of Education in the provisional government and on the Executive Committee; his democratic bill on popular education was a lively protest against the law on education owed to the Jesuits. These three candidates represented the three allied classes: in front, the insurrecto of June, the representative of the revolutionary proletariat; beside him, the doctrinaire socialist, the representative of the socialist petty bourgeoisie; the third, finally, the representative of the bourgeois republican party, whose democratic formulas, in the face of the party of order, acquired a socialist meaning, and had long since lost their proper meaning. It was, as in February, a general coalition against the bourgeoisie and the Government. But this time the proletariat was at the head of the revolutionary league.

Despite all efforts, the socialist candidates triumphed. The army itself voted for the June insurgent, against its own Minister of War, Lahittte. The party of order was as if struck by lightning. The elections in the departments were of no consolation to it: their result was a majority of montagnards. The election of March 10, 18501 It was the negation of June 1848: the massacriers and the "deporteurs" of the June rebels were back in the National Assembly, spine bowed, behind the deportees and their contemptuous principles. It was the negation of June 13, 1849: La Montagne, proscribed by the National Assembly, was back in the National Assembly, but as the advanced bugler of the revolution and no longer its leader. It was the negation of December 10: Napoleon had suffered a setback with his minister Lahitte. The parliamentary history of France knows only one analogous case: the failure of Haussez, Charles X's minister, in 1830. The election of March 10, 1850 finally annulled that of May 13, which had given the majority to the party of order. The election of March 10 protested against the majority of May 13. March 10 was a revolution. Behind the ballot papers, the unexpected defeat.

"The March 10 vote is war," cried Ségur dAguesseau, one of

the most prominent members of the order party.

With March 10, 1850, the constitutional Republic enters a new phase, the phase of its dissolution. The different fractions of the majority are again united among themselves and with Bonaparte. They are again the gentlemen of order and he is again their neutral man. When they remember that they are monarchists, it is only because they have no more hope in the possibility of the bourgeois republic; he, when he remembers that he is the president, it is only because he has no hope of remaining so.

To the election of Deflotte, the rebel of June, Bonaparte responds, on the nomination of the party of order, with the appointment of Baroche as minister of the interior; Baroche, the accuser of Blanqui and of Barbês, of Ledru-Rollin and of Guinard. To the election of Carnot, the Legislative responds with the vote for the law on education; to the election of Vidal, with the strangling of the Socialist press. By the "trumpets" of its press, the party of order seeks to dispel its own fear. "The sword is sacred," cries one of its organs. "It is necessary that the defenders of order take the offensive against the red party," says another. "Between socialism and society there is a duel of death, a merciless, unrelenting war; in this desperate duel, one or the other must disappear, if society does not annul socialism, socialism will annul society," chants a third order rooster. Raise the barricades of order, the barricades of religion! We must break with the one hundred and twenty-seven thousand voters of Paris! A Saint Bartholomew of the socialists! And the party of order believed for an instant in the certainty of its own victory. It is against the "merchants of Paris" that its organs struggle in the most fanatical manner. The rebel of June, elected representative of the merchants of Paris! This means that a second June 1848 is impossible, this means that a second June 13, 1849 is impossible, this means that the moral influence of capital has been destroyed, this means that the bourgeois Assembly represents only the bourgeoisie, this means that large property is lost, for its vassal, small property, seeks its salvation in the camp of the non-capitalists.

The party of order inevitably returns to its commonplace: "Greater repression!" it exclaims, "ten times more repression!"; but its power of repression is ten times weaker, while resistance is a hundred times stronger. The chief instrument of repression, the army, must it not be called to its senses? And the party of order utters its last words: "It is necessary to break the iron circle of a suffocating legality. The constitutional Republic is impossible. It is necessary that we fight with our real weapons: after February 1848, we have fought the Revolution with its weapons and within its terrain; we accept its institutions, the Constitution is a fortress that protects the attackers, not the attacked. Hiding in the belly of the Trojan horse, in the holy Ilium, imitating our ancestors, the Greeks, we did not conquer the enemy city, we were made, on the contrary, ourselves, the prisoners."

But the foundation of the Constitution is universal suffrage. The suppression of universal suffrage will be the last word of the party of order, of the bourgeois dictatorship.

Universal suffrage proved him right on May 24, 1848, on December 20, 1848, on May 13, 1849, on July 8, 1849. Universal suffrage undermined itself on March 10, 1850. Bourgeois domination, as an emanation and result of universal suffrage, as the expression of the will of the sovereign people, this is the meaning of the bourgeois constitution. But from the moment that the content of this right to suffrage, of this sovereign will is no longer bourgeois domination, will the Constitution still have a meaning? Is it not the duty of the bourgeoisie to regulate the right to vote in such a way that it accepts the reasonable, is its domination? Universal suffrage, constantly suppressing again the reigning public power, and making it emanate again from its bosom, does it not suppress all stability, does it not every instant call into question all established powers, does it not annul authority, does it not threaten to make authority itself anarchy? After March 10, who could still doubt? Rejecting universal suffrage, in which it had hitherto involved itself, and from which it drew all its omnipotence, the bourgeoisie bluntly confesses, "Our victory has been maintained up to this point by the will of the people; it must now be consolidated against the will of the people." And, in a consequent manner, it seeks its supports no longer in France, but outside of it, abroad, in the invasion.

With the invasion, according to Coblence, having established its headquarters in France itself, it raises all national passions against it. With its attack on universal suffrage, it provides the new revolution with a general pretext; and the revolution needs such a pretext. Any particular pretext would separate the fractions of the revolutionary league and bring out their differences. The general pretext stuns the semi-revolutionary classes; it allows them to delude themselves about the determined character of the coming revolution, about the consequences of their own action. Every revolution needs a "banquet affair." Universal suffrage is the "banqueting affair" of the new revolution.

But the coalition of bourgeois factions is already doomed when it takes refuge outside the only possible form of its common power, the most powerful and most complete form of its class domination, the constitutional republic, and towards the inferior, incomplete and weakest form of the monarchy. They resemble the old man who, in order to regain his youthful strength, goes back to wearing his childhood clothes and tries, badly, to hide his shriveled limbs. The Republic of coalesced bourgeois fractions has only one merit, that of being the hothouse of the revolution.

The March 10, 1850 carries the headline:

"After me, the flood."

Printed in Great Britain
by Amazon

65921703R00061